THE PUBLIC LIBRARY DIRECTOR'S TOOLKIT

THE **PUBLIC LIBRARY DIRECTOR'S** TOOLKIT

KATE HALL | KATHY PARKER

ALA Editions

CHICAGO | 2019

KATE HALL has been a library director since 2010, first at New Lenox and now at Northbrook Public Library in Illinois. After nearly twenty years in libraries, Kate has held numerous library leadership positions and has worked with Kathy Parker on the successful Director's University program that has taught more than 100 new library directors what they need to know to run a library. Kate is active on many boards, including serving previously on the Illinois Library Association Executive Board and as President on the Board of Directors for the Reaching Across Illinois Library System.

KATHY PARKER has more than thirty-five years of library experience, with sixteen years serving as library director at Glenwood–Lynwood Public Library in Illinois. Kathy has participated on various regional library boards, served as a library trustee at her local library and in the regional library system, and was the recipient of the American Library Association Trustee Citation in 2016. She values the importance of lifelong learning and has started several continuing education initiatives for library staff and trustees. Kathy retired in summer 2018 and has started her own consulting business, serving as an interim director, offering coaching to new directors and providing development to boards.

© 2019 by the American Library Association

Extensive effort has gone into ensuring the reliability of the information in this book; however, the publisher makes no warranty, express or implied, with respect to the material contained herein.

ISBN: 978-0-8389-1859-3 (paper)

Library of Congress Cataloging-in-Publication Data
Names: Hall, Kate, 1979– author. | Parker, Kathy, 1963– author.
Title: The public library director's toolkit / Kate Hall and Kathy Parker.
Description: Chicago : ALA Editions, 2019. | Includes index.
Identifiers: LCCN 2018055828 | ISBN 9780838918593 (print : alk. paper)
Subjects: LCSH: Library directors—United States—Handbook, manuals, etc. | Public libraries—
    United States—Administration—Handbook, manuals, etc.
Classification: LCC Z682.4.A34 H35 2019 | DDC 025.1/970092—dc23
LC record available at https://lccn.loc.gov/2018055828

Cover design by Kim Thornton. Image © jakkapan / Adobe Stock.
Text design and composition by Karen Sheets de Gracia in the Gotham and Mercury typefaces.

♾ This paper meets the requirements of ANSI/NISO Z39.48–1992 (Permanence of Paper).

PRINTED IN THE UNITED STATES OF AMERICA
23 22 21 20 19   5 4 3 2 1

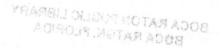

To my mother for helping me grow into who I am today;
to my favorite sister, Elizabeth, for keeping me grounded;
and to my husband for always encouraging my dreams
—KH

To my parents who taught me that anything is possible if you work hard;
to my grandmother who always wanted to write a book
and instilled that same dream in me early on;
and to my family and friends who have always supported
and loved me unconditionally
—KP

CONTENTS

ACKNOWLEDGMENTS

WE WOULD LIKE to thank everyone who made this book possible.

To our wonderful editor at ALA Editions, Jamie Santoro, who took a chance on us.

To the Oak Brook (IL) Public Library for providing us with a meeting place to collaborate on this book.

To our beta readers, Kelly Durov and Courtney Young, who helped us make this book relevant to aspiring and current directors. Your insight was invaluable.

To our guinea pigs, who agreed to read through our first draft and helped us spot the areas that needed polishing: Dee Brennan, Susan Dienes, Joseph Filapek, Andy Kim, Laurie Prioletti, and Cindy Rauch.

To the board members and staff at the Glenwood–Lynwood Public Library District, New Lenox Public Library District, and Northbrook Public Library, who continue to inspire us to become the best directors and librarians we can be.

And, finally, to our colleagues, past and present, and the entire library world we get to interact with every day. We are proud to be part of this community of lifelong learners.

INTRODUCTION

RUNNING A LIBRARY is a big task, with many moving parts. Staff, patrons, boards, community meetings, legal and financial requirements, professional demands—where do you go for help?

When we started out as library directors, there was so much we didn't know. We learned by trial and error, calling on our colleagues, attorneys, and other professionals more times than we could count—because there was no one source to answer all our questions. That is why we are writing this book. We do not want future librarians, management staff and trustees to be as bewildered as we were when we became public library directors. We love libraries and want to see them succeed. In order to do that, directors need to have certain tools in their toolkit. We want to provide those tools and help you come up with your own toolkit that you can use as a library director.

As with any administrative-level position, it will take about a year to learn the basic responsibilities. We will take you through the core components of what you need to know, help you skip some of the pain points that we both went through, and provide resources that you can use in your work. The book is divided into two parts: part I gives you an overview of the basic responsibilities of being a public library director, and part II provides sample documents and forms that you can use immediately.

Let the journey begin.

PART I
DIRECTOR TOOLBOX

1

GETTING STARTED

After reading this chapter, you will know the following:

- What the basic responsibilities for being a public library director are
- How to set yourself up for success your first day, week, month, and year
- How to gather the information you need to be successful
- How to put together a communication strategy
- How to set up systems to maintain harmony between work and your personal life

S tarting a new job is exhilarating, but it can also be daunting. Starting as a director only intensifies those feelings. Starting at a new library as director means you are supposed to take charge, but you don't necessarily know all the processes and past history on how things have been handled at this library. We will go through the steps you can take to set yourself up for success from day one.

CORE RESPONSIBILITIES

What exactly are your responsibilities? Depending on the size of library you work in, this could mean anything from making sure the doors are unlocked at opening to overseeing managers who have staff who carry out the core functions of the library. You may actively perform the following duties or oversee other staff who perform them, but, ultimately, the buck stops with you, so you want to be aware of what is going on in your building.

PERSONNEL

You are ultimately responsible for the hiring, training, supervision, evaluation, and, if necessary, termination of all the employees at the library. Depending on your library's size, you may do all of these tasks yourself, have managers who hire their own staff, or perhaps even have an HR (human resources) manager or department that does the hiring.

BOARD OF TRUSTEES

The library director reports to the board, and thus should cultivate a good working relationship with board members, but is also responsible for ensuring the board is educated on the library's finances, its strategic plan, and the programs and services the library provides. You are in charge of creating the monthly board packet and delivering information to your board.

FINANCES

Preparing the budget for the board's review and approval is one of your key functions. This includes planning ahead to ensure that you have enough money for building repairs, staff raises, and technology improvements as well as presenting monthly reports to the board about the library's finances. You are responsible for making sure the budget is being spent appropriately and for creating the monthly financial statements. Sometimes this means you are actually running the report, but you may instead have a business manager or outside accounting firm that prepares the statements and creates the checks for you.

LEGAL MATTERS

Any legal concerns will go through the director. Legal matters can include working with the attorney to draft new policies, review contracts, or handle personnel issues. The library director should be the main point of contact for the library attorney and is in charge of ensuring the library is complying with all applicable laws.

POLICIES AND PROCEDURES

Having strong policies and procedures helps create a well-run library. While the board approves policies, the library director is responsible for crafting the policies and procedures that help run the library.

INSURANCE

There are many types of insurance, which is covered in more detail in chapter 7. The director manages the insurance the library provides and ensures the library building and staff are adequately covered.

BUILDING MAINTENANCE

The physical maintenance of your building is also up to you. Depending on the size of your building and your type of library, this could mean different things. Some libraries may have paid maintenance staff, or the director may be the maintenance staff. However maintenance is handled in your library, the director has to be aware of all aspects of the building so that informed decisions can be made when necessary.

EMERGENCY PLANNING

As director, not only do you handle the day-to-day emergencies that pop up at a library, but you also must prepare for larger emergencies. Creating an emergency plan and ensuring staff are trained to react appropriately to emergencies is an essential piece of the director's job.

COLLECTION DEVELOPMENT

Depending on the size of the library and staff, the director may or may not be the person doing collection development. Either way, the director is ultimately responsible for making sure that the library collection is current, sufficient, and representative of the community's wants and needs. This means making sure there is sufficient funding for new materials, evaluating new types of items to add to the collection, and ensuring that weeding is happening on a regular basis.

PROGRAMMING AND SERVICES

As the director, you are ultimately responsible for making sure that the library is offering a diverse range of programs and services to meet the wants and needs of the community. You also need to determine what services the library may want to provide. In order to find out what your community wants, they need to be queried.

COMMUNITY ENGAGEMENT

You should attend community outreach events and be active in local organizations like Rotary, Kiwanis, Lions, and so forth. By being active and getting to know the community, you can better advocate for the role of the library in that community.

TECHNOLOGY

Taking care of the facility means ensuring you have appropriate technologies in place for staff and patrons. Ensuring that you have the technology your community needs and planning for future costs are responsibilities of the director. You will also need to set and enforce technology competencies for staff and stay up-to-date on technology issues and trends.

STRATEGIC PLAN

In order to know why you do what you do, you need to have a clear mission and vision. The board sets the strategic plan, but it is the director's job to carry out the directives of that plan.

YOUR FIRST YEAR

Now that you know your responsibilities, how do you do the job?

FIRST DAY

First, prep yourself. Read the board minutes and board packets, if you have access to them, and the library policies, personnel policies, and any other recent information you can obtain about the library, including recent news articles, online reviews, and so on, before your first day. Ideally, this was part of your interview preparation, but if not, do it now. This will give you an idea of what issues you might be facing in your first few days, weeks, and months at your library. Focus on reading policies that you might have to use right away, like the patron behavior policy or unattended children policy. Make a list of all the things that you think you will need to learn. You will need to become your own trainer. Check out part II, "Tools," for a recommended list of training topics to help you get started.

Second, admit when you don't know something and ask for background information for clarification. Not knowing everything when you start a job is to be expected. Asking for help will enable you to gather as much information as possible to help you make better decisions for the library. It also shows your staff that even the boss needs to ask for help sometimes, and it is healthy to do so. Depending on library size, you might have an administrative team or it might be just you and one or two other people. Go to the administrative or management team to gain background on issues or topics as they arise. If yours is a smaller library, you can ask the other staff members for information. Asking your board president for information can also be useful, depending on the relationship the board had with the previous director.

FIRST WEEK

After you make it through your first day, you can focus on your first week. You aren't expected to have everything down pat, and you will have some flexibility in your schedule. Use this freedom to your advantage to gain insight into your library's workings.

Tour the library each day and look at it through the eyes of a patron. Note the things that work well. Then turn your focus to areas that you would like to eventually change:

- What strikes you as discordant or odd in the layout, workflow, or signage?
- What procedures and processes seem to be cumbersome or unfriendly?
- Are there any workflows, procedures, or processes that could be adjusted?

While you are still new to the library, you are able to see the library in a different light. Keep a file on what changes you think need to be made in the future to make the library more accessible for the community and for staff. Share with staff what you see as working well so you are not just focusing on all the things you want to change. For the moment, just jot down what you want to change; don't actually make the changes. Give yourself time to learn about the library and community before committing to any changes.

The first week is also a good time to start to get to know your direct reports. Schedule one-on-one sessions with each of your managers to get to know them a little better. Have a set of questions that you ask each one so that you can get a well-rounded picture of the people in your library. You may not be able to meet with everyone in the first week, but getting a few such meetings under your belt will set you up for success in the long run. Here are some suggestions for questions you can ask your managers:

- What is your background?
- What are you passionate about?
- What current projects are you and/or your department working on?
- What do you wish you could do individually, as a department, or for the entire library?
- Do you have anything you would like to see changed or anything you have an issue with?
- How do you prefer to communicate (phone, e-mail, face-to-face)?
- What are the biggest challenges the library is facing (or will face in the near future)?
- Why is the library going to face these challenges?
- What are the most promising unexploited opportunities for improvement?
- What would need to happen for the library to exploit the potential of these opportunities?
- If you were leading the library, on what would you focus your attention?

Next, set up some meet-and-greets with the remainder of the staff. If you have a smaller staff, meeting with them one-on-one would be great. If your staff is larger, this may be more difficult. You can use some of the questions that you asked your managers to dig into what motivates staff as well as uncover issues that you may need to address, areas for improvement, and sources of staff pride.

When you are not meeting with people or touring the library, take time to set yourself up for success in your work environment. Ask yourself these questions to help you create an environment that will work best for you:

- What tools and supplies do I need to help me be successful and stay on top of my to-do list?
- What setup do I need to have to work at peak efficiency? (Where should my computer go? My desk? Visitor's chair? File cabinet?)
- What kind of environment do I want to create in my office? (Will I hang pictures on the wall? Will I have any personal items in my office?)
- What message do I want to send to staff, vendors, board members, and others about the type of director I am based on how my office appears?

TAKE A BREAK

Don't forget to take breaks! In 2011, a study at the University of Illinois at Urbana–Champaign found that even brief breaks from a task can dramatically improve your ability to focus on that task for prolonged periods.*

———

*Atsunori Ariga and Alejandro Lleras, "Brief and Rare Mental 'Breaks' Keep You Focused: Deactivation and Reactivation of Task Goals Preempt Vigilance Decrements." Cognition 118, no. 3 (March 2011): 439–43, doi:10.1016/j.cognition.2010.12.007.

Your workspace conveys in a glance what you are about so you want to make sure it reflects you at your best.

The first week can be exhausting. Not only are you meeting with many new people; you are also trying to absorb significant amounts of information on policies, procedures, and millions of other pieces of data you are gathering. Don't feel that you have to learn everything in a week. When you go home at night, rest and do something unrelated to the library. This allows you a chance to process all the information you have received that day.

FIRST MONTH

In your first week, you hopefully set up some times to meet with your managers and staff. But chances are you did not get all of that done in that one week. Use the rest of the month to meet with those people and also with other key people in the community. Go to the village/city hall, schools, park district, chamber of commerce, and so forth, and introduce yourself. Take time to meet with each board member one-on-one, if you can, and ask them about their vision for the library and the future. Hopefully, your library will have a strategic plan that will help guide you on where the library is headed. If not, turn to chapter 11 for information on how to craft a strategic plan for your library.

One critical activity to do during your first month is to walk around your library every day to say hello to people and chat for a few minutes with staff and patrons. Not only will this help you learn the flow of your library and become familiar with the building itself; it will also give people a chance to know you. Building relationships early on will help you understand what motivates people and give you a better sense of your community's interests and your staff's skills and abilities. This knowledge will help you down the road when it comes time to assign people to projects or to help get buy-in on new initiatives.

One of the main components of setting yourself up for future success is to develop a communication strategy. Creating a plan during your first month will help set the tone for how you share information with the staff, board, and community. Ask yourself these questions:

- What is my vision for a great library? How will I convey that to staff and the board?
- What processes do I want to put in place to communicate with staff and with the board?
- How often should I communicate with staff? How will I convey general information in addition to larger project information?
- How often does the board expect updates and reports? How do board members prefer to receive that type of information?

Set up a schedule that delineates how, when, and what you will communicate with staff. This might mean weekly meetings with managers, quarterly all-staff meetings, and/or monthly e-mails reporting on what is going on in the library. What, when, and how you choose to communicate will depend on the size and culture of your library. Figuring out a plan now will ensure that you don't lose track of time and find yourself a year into the job with staff telling you that they never know what is going on in the library.

You should also set up a plan to communicate with board members, based on their preferences. Some boards may be fine with the monthly director's report in the board packet along with the occasional e-mail when an important issue arises, and other boards might prefer more frequent communication. Discuss what types of information board members prefer and how often they expect to receive it from you.

During your first month, you will also have your first board meeting. Hopefully, you attended some of the board meetings before you became director or attended them at your previous library. If not, don't worry. The hardest part of the monthly board meeting is not the meeting, but the preparation of the board packet for the meeting. With luck, the library has an assistant director, business manager, or administrative assistant to help you through this process. If not, contact a colleague to ask how to put together the packet or, at the very least, look at the previous packets to see what is normally included. That first board meeting is an excellent opportunity to query the board members about their preferred method and frequency of communication. Start by working with the board president to draft agenda items. Then, look at what the board discussed during that month in previous years. Learn more about putting together a board packet in chapter 3, where you can also check out a timeline for typical board meeting agenda items.

For the first few months, don't make any dramatic changes to the agenda, reports, or statistics. Get to know the board members a bit and let them get to know you and your style before introducing any changes. Having read the packets from previous board meetings, you should have a general idea of what is included. The following standard parts typically appear in each packet:

- *Agenda:* This lists everything you will be discussing at the meeting.
- *Minutes:* These describe the activity during the previous month's meeting and should hopefully be done before the new meeting.
- *Financial statements:* Each month you will include a snapshot of your library's finances, including a list of all the bills and charges for the previous month.
- *Director's report:* This is a summary of what you have done, what the library has done, and sometimes what actions have been taken on specific items from the strategic plan. You will find a director's report template in part II, "Tools."
- *Statistics:* This section comprises the overall stats of the library. It may include programming attendance, circulation, and so on, and may also be accompanied by patron stories.

Some documents (e.g., budget, contracts, and reports) in the packet will depend on what you have listed on the agenda each month. Most states will also have a timeline for required actions that the library must take each year. Check with your state library, library system, or attorney to find out what the requirements are in your area.

Finally, reach out to your neighboring libraries and meet or at least talk to the other directors. They can become an invaluable network for you when you issues or problems come up. They are also a great source for inspiration and can serve as a sounding board for ideas and problems. Being a director can be lonely because there are certain things you cannot talk about with your staff. Having a strong peer network will provide you with an outlet to vent frustrations, an avenue for problem solving, and a source of understanding.

FIRST YEAR

To really understand all of the ins and outs of being a director, you will need to experience a twelve-month cycle. The year has a certain rhythm to it that will help you understand the flow of the library. Make sure you know what your fiscal year start and end dates are. Keep in mind that certain times of year are busier and will require more forethought and planning.

During your first year, take time to jot down important events that happen annually, monthly, semiannually, and so on. Here are some events that will repeat:

- Board meetings
- Staff meetings (including staff development days)
- Meetings for library consortia or systems
- Networking group meetings
- School and other community visits that the library participates in
- Outreach events in the community
- Events hosted by the chamber of commerce and other organizations
- Annual holiday parties

By keeping track of events as they happen, you can build a calendar that will help you structure your time and prevent events from sneaking up on you.

During this time, you will also get to know your vendors. With whom do you contract? Where are the contracts? What services do the vendors provide? Reach out to regular vendors to meet them and get to know about their services.

WORK AND PERSONAL LIFE HARMONY

If you start out by looking toward the future, you can build a strong foundation for success at work. But the other key component to success is maintaining a good balance between your work and your personal life. In addition to taking breaks at work, you need to make sure you are maintaining balance in your entire life to help you create a harmonious life.

There will be times when you have a large project to complete or a pressing personnel issue to resolve, but you need to be cautious of letting your job consume your entire life. You are in charge, and you will feel overwhelmed at times. The best way to combat that is to make sure you have good systems in place in your personal life so you don't burn out. While as library director you are never really "off" duty because of the responsibilities you carry, it is possible to turn off the switch and manage your time.

But how? Technology plays a major role in our lives today, and while it can make life more efficient, it can also make you too accessible. If you feel that you need to be available 24/7, your brain won't have a chance to reset and rest. Create boundaries that will work for you to maintain balance between work demands and your need for downtime. You need to consider what will work for you. Here are some suggestions:

- Turn off notifications for e-mail on your phone and tablet.
- Refrain from doing work on weekends.
- Don't take paperwork or journals home with you. Make time to read them at work.
- Set up your schedule so you can accomplish work at work; make sure you have time on your calendar to follow up on items after meetings.
- Make some "you" time daily, whether it is practicing meditation, reading a book, listening to music, or watching TV.
- When you are off (weekends, holidays, vacations), train your staff to contact you only in emergency situations (after they call 911).

At the beginning, you may feel like you need to attend every meeting and continuing education event or participate whenever someone asks you. This is natural since you are in a learning phase and want to be engaged. Until you have a good handle on your workload, try to defer any requests for your involvement in different libraries. Don't take on more than you can handle; learn to take on what is reasonable. Keep track of how much time you spend on different tasks so you can get a sense of where you are spending your energy. If one area is consuming a lot of your time, consider what you can stop doing or delegate to someone else. You will have time to take on more commitments as you get more familiar with your responsibilities.

It is not easy to create boundaries, and most library directors will overextend themselves at some point in their careers. There will be times when creating harmony between work and personal life seems impossible, but keeping the need for boundaries in the forefront of your mind will help you be more committed and productive at work and at home.

✿ REVIEW AND REFLECT

KEY TAKEAWAYS

A director has many responsibilities. Most of them fall into these core areas:

- Personnel
- Board of trustees

- Finances
- Legal matters
- Policies and procedures
- Insurance
- Building maintenance
- Emergency planning
- Collection development
- Programming and services
- Community engagement
- Technology
- Strategic plan

Setting yourself up for success over the course of your first year includes

- walking through your building regularly;
- meeting with staff, board, and community members;
- creating a training plan for yourself;
- jotting down key dates and events;
- organizing your office and files; and
- pacing yourself so you don't become overwhelmed.

Remember that all work and no play is no good for anyone. Creating balance in your life is critical to being an effective director.

SELF-CHECK

- Have I read background information like board packets and policies and other information about the library?
- Have I created a training checklist for myself?
- Have I scheduled one-on-one sessions with managers, staff, and board members?
- What current projects are under way or about to begin?
- Based on feedback and observation, what areas of the library do I need to address immediately? In my first year? Someday?
- Have I started a calendar of library-wide and community meetings and events?
- Do I have the tools and supplies I need to help me be successful?

QUESTIONS FOR REFLECTION

- What is the best way for me to communicate with managers, staff, and the board?
- Whom do I have in my network now that I can turn to for help?

- What tasks do I need to do? What tasks can I delegate to someone else?
- What kind of communication do I want to provide for my staff, board members, and the community?
- How can I set clear boundaries to ensure I don't burn out?
- Do I have the optimum setup for my office to help me achieve peak efficiency and convey the type of director I want to be?
- How can I maintain harmony between my work and my personal life?

ADDITIONAL RESOURCES

See part II for these additional resources on starting work as a library director:

- Sample 1.1: Library Director Training Checklist
- Sample 1.2: Director's Report Template

⤓ **Download additional resources on our website at www.librarydirectorstoolkit.com/resources.**

Allen, D. *Getting Things Done: The Art of Stress-Free Productivity*. London: Penguin Books, 2002.

Brandt, G. *The New Leader's 100-Day Action Plan: How to Take Charge, Build or Merge Your Team, and Get Immediate Results*. Hoboken, NJ: Wiley, 2016.

Collins, J. *Good to Great: Why Some Companies Make the Leap and Others Don't*. New York: Harper Business, 2001.

Daly, P., M. Watkins, and C. Reavis. *First 90 Days in Government: Critical Success Strategies for New Public Managers at All Levels*. Boston, MA: Harvard Business Review Press, 2006.

Drucker, P. *Effective Executive: The Definitive Guide to Getting the Right Things Done*. New York: Harper Business, 2017.

Hakala-Ausperk, C. *Be a Great Boss: One Year to Success*. Chicago: American Library Association, 2011.

2

EMPLOYEES

After reading this chapter, you will know the following:

- How to hire an employee, including creating a job description and job advertisement, interviewing, and checking references
- How to onboard an employee
- Why you need a salary schedule
- How to train employees and provide feedback
- How to be aware of the legal aspects of HR (human resources)
- Why you need a personnel policy manual
- How to effectively discipline and separate an employee from the library

E mployees are the cornerstone of any library. They are the face of the library, the ones who interact with the public and account for the largest portion of a library's budget. Investing in employees is investing in the library. Hiring, training, and managing staff are some of the most important and time-consuming parts of the library director's job. It is important to have staff who are customer service oriented, knowledgeable, dependable, and a good fit for the culture of the library and community. In order to accomplish this, the library must be deliberate in the decision-making process to hire and keep employees who are engaged in their work and continual learning journey.

JOB DESCRIPTIONS

Before you can hire employees, you will need to compile a list of tasks for which they will be responsible. In addition, job descriptions should tell employees whether they are exempt or nonexempt (see table 2.1). Good job descriptions give employees an idea of what is expected of them in their positions and are important in the hiring process, the evaluation process, and the termination process.

Job descriptions should be evaluated regularly to ensure currency and accuracy of the position's responsibilities. Each time a position opens up, take that opportunity to revise the job description. If a position does not have a lot of turnover, review the job description every three to five years to ensure it stays up-to-date. Remember that a job advertisement and a job description are two different things. The job description is the general explanation of what the job entails, while the job advertisement announces the position's availability to the public and interested parties and shares the position's responsibilities and culture of the library.

A typical job description should include basic position information, a job summary, the necessary qualifications, essential job functions, and information on working conditions.

POSITION INFORMATION

- Title
- Department
- To whom the employee reports
- When the job description was last updated

TABLE 2.1 Exempt versus Nonexempt

EXEMPT	NONEXEMPT
Salaried	Paid hourly (no less than federal minimum wage) or salaried
Works hours necessary to complete essential functions (can be more or less than regular full-time week)	Works scheduled hours
Tracks time but has a flexible schedule	Tracks time and has little flexibility in determining schedule
No overtime pay after forty hours	Overtime pay beyond forty hours
Considered less generous under federal law	Considered more generous under federal law
Must meet FLSA standards to qualify as exempt	Can apply to any employee
Can collect unemployment benefits	Can collect unemployment benefits

- Optional items: full time/part time, Fair Labor Standards Act (FLSA) code, and job grade, if applicable

JOB SUMMARY

The job summary should be only one to two sentences in length and provide the job overview, including the general nature and purpose of the position. Here is an example of a librarian job summary: Under the supervision of the Adult Services Manager, this employee is responsible for providing reference and readers' advisory services, participating in collection development, and planning and presenting programs.

QUALIFICATIONS

Qualifications include the minimum level of education, experience, skills, and abilities a person must possess in order to do the job. Here is an example of qualifications required for a children's librarian position:

- Master of Library and Information Science degree from an American Library Association (ALA)–accredited school
- Experience working with children and working knowledge of infant, child, and adolescent development
- Basic computer skills
- Ability to communicate clearly and effectively and establish and maintain effective working relationships with staff
- Ability to work independently and productively
- Ability to develop and effectively use reference skills and practices
- Thorough knowledge of general library philosophy, including the Library Bill of Rights
- Ability to transform that knowledge into daily practice in the fulfillment of responsibilities
- Working knowledge of library computer software systems and ability to problem solve and troubleshoot same
- Working knowledge of the recreational reading interests and curriculum-related information needs of children, preschool through young adult, and their parents/caregivers

ESSENTIAL JOB FUNCTIONS

Essential job functions are the fundamental duties of a position. This section should not be used to list every single task a person does but should instead provide a broad overview of the position's duties, ranked from most important to least important. Here are some examples of a librarian's essential job functions:

1. Provide reference/readers' advisory services using digital and print resources.
2. Instruct and assist patrons in the selection and use of resources.
3. Select materials in designated buying areas. Remove damaged or outdated materials from the collection.
4. Plan, present, and assist with the production of programs to meet the reading/discussion needs of adults.
5. Develop and provide services and outreach to special population groups.
6. Create displays, bibliographies, brochures, program promotions, and website material.
7. Keep informed of current trends and professional techniques; participate in professional organizations.
8. Perform other related duties as assigned.

WORKING CONDITIONS

The working conditions are the last item covered in the job description. This section lists the physical requirements for the position, including minimum and maximum time limits and lift-and-carry weights, if necessary. Here is an example of a working conditions section:

- Duties are performed indoors in an office environment.
- Duties require extended periods of standing, walking, sitting, and talking or hearing for a minimum of four hours.
- Duties require occasional periods of climbing or balancing, pulling/ pushing items, lifting/carrying items, keyboarding, reaching with hands and arms, stooping, kneeling, crouching, or crawling for a minimum of fifteen-minute intervals.
- Duties require lifting up to fifty pounds; bending, stooping, and climbing; pushing and/or pulling wheeled items up to seventy-five pounds; reaching; and handling and fine manipulation skills.
- Vision requirements include close vision and ability to adjust focus.
- The noise level is usually moderate.
- Applicant must be able to transport self to work-related meetings, workshops, conferences, and so forth.

HIRING PROCESS

JOB ADVERTISEMENT

Now that you have a solid job description, it is time to write the job advertisement. The job advertisement is critical to finding candidates for the open position. Hiring well is an essential component to the library's success. According to Gallup, companies fail to choose the candidate with the right talent for the job 82 percent of the time.[1] This poll focused on management positions, so this is a terrifying number because it means that most organizations don't have managers in place who can make good hiring decisions and who perhaps are not suited for their own roles as managers.

The hiring process begins when the job advertisement is posted. This is the first impression that prospective candidates will have of the library and will help to determine if they would be a good fit for the library. Make sure the job advertisement represents the library's culture and isn't just a listing of the position's duties. Is the library relaxed and casual or more formal and business focused? Imbue your job advertisement with the spirit of your library to help candidates get a sense of what working at your library is like. The ad should also include information about the salary range and basic benefits package.

INTERVIEW PROCESS

After receiving applications, review them to determine whom you want to interview. Create a set of questions to ask every applicant. Questions should provide answers that will help you make an unbiased decision about whom to hire based on applicants' skills and abilities and also determine how well each applicant would fit in with the library's culture. Avoid asking any questions about disabilities, medical information, marital status, sexual orientation, religion, and place of residence. Questions should be focused on learning about how well applicants can perform the essential job functions. Don't ask yes-or-no questions. Ask experiential questions and others that will highlight critical-thinking abilities. Here are some examples:

- Why are you interested in this position?
- Describe how previous experience makes you qualified for this position.
- Describe how you would handle . . . [*insert scenario*].
- Describe a time when you had to deal with a difficult patron.

If possible, invite another person, such as a manager or other key staff member, to be part of the interview process. This will provide feedback about the candidate from another source and allow you to observe the interactions between the candidate and a current staff member. After each interview is finished, write up a summary of overall impressions about the candidate based on the notes taken during the interview. Summarizing your thoughts will help you to make the decision about whom to hire.

CANDIDATE REFERENCES

Once you have selected the candidate you would like to hire, contact that applicant's references. The interview is just one face of the candidate. Contacting references will give a larger picture of the candidate. As with an interview, you should prepare a set of specific questions to ask of all the references. Here are some examples of topics to cover:

- Overall impression of the candidate and the history of their relationship
- Quality of the candidate's work
- Whether the reference would rehire the candidate
- What the candidate's strengths and areas of improvement are
- Specific questions about how the reference thinks the candidate would handle different parts of the job

After the references have been vetted, you are ready to offer the position to the preferred candidate. The written job offer should include the salary and specific benefits for the position.

COMPENSATION

How does the library determine the salary for the position? Compensation is possibly the most critical portion of hiring, evaluating, and handling personnel. Yet it is something that many don't understand. How are salaries and salary increases determined? It all starts with a salary schedule.

A salary schedule is a listing of salary ranges by title, department, position, or grade, and it is the key to developing and maintaining a fair compensation package for your library. A salary schedule is created through a compensation benchmarking process. This benchmarking process compares job descriptions to established salary survey jobs in order to identify the appropriate salary for a position.

Why does a library need a salary schedule? A solid salary schedule will help the library

- attract, retain, and motivate employees;
- remain externally competitive;
- be fair and equitable in awarding compensation;
- comply with local, state, and federal laws; and
- be cost-effective.

A salary compensation and benchmarking project usually has a shelf life of about three to five years, with the appropriate annual cost-of-living updates. However—and this is the critical piece—you will need to validate the compensation rates of key jobs, hard-to-fill jobs, and any position with high turnover. These might include jobs in areas like information technology (IT), graphic design, or makerspaces or newer positions.

Any new positions added after the compensation study will also need to be benchmarked to determine the appropriate pay grade. If this service is outsourced, an HR consulting firm will typically charge a flat rate for a single job description. Any

HR consulting firm that does the study should also provide at least three years of updates to the salary schedule based on any market changes.

ONBOARDING

Now that you have a new hire, the rest of the work is about to begin. We discuss the importance of networking and continuing education in chapter 12, but know that everything starts with the onboarding process. To begin, you should create a checklist of all the HR-related functions the new hire must complete. Check out part II, "Tools," for an example of an onboarding checklist.

Once the new hires have completed the HR tasks, you should provide them with a separate onboarding checklist specific to the responsibilities for their position. The checklists for managers tend to be more self-directed, whereas a new circulation clerk might engage in more one-on-one training with a manager, a supervisor, or coworkers. Whatever the position, be sure to give new hires a list with a timeline (if possible) of what they are going to learn and from whom and when.

Remember that new hires will be processing a lot of new information and will need time to absorb that information. Be sure they have a grasp on one idea or task before introducing them to more.

PERSONNEL POLICIES

Whether your organization calls it a personnel manual or an employee handbook, be sure the document is up-to-date. Give all new hires a copy of the personnel manual and have them sign a document indicating that they have received, read, and understood the policies. This lets them know that you expect them to have an understanding of the policies and to behave accordingly. Such documentation can come in handy when you are faced with a disciplinary issue.

Personnel policies are used to help define the library's culture and environment and to ensure staff are treated consistently. Many policies are mandated by federal, state, or local law, and these should be included in your manual. Policies are discussed in more detail in chapter 6.

The policy manual should be kept current. Be sure to do a cursory review annually and a full-scale update every three to four years. When crafting a personnel policy, add anything that is "understood" by everyone but not written down. If it is "understood" that the day before Thanksgiving is treated as a half day of work for staff, this should be in the policy. If staff are allowed to take longer lunches with approval from their manager if they make it up during the week, this should be in the policy. Clear documentation helps ensure that there will be fewer problems in the future. Sometimes something happens that will cause you to sit up and take notice and realize that there is no policy to cover the situation. A policy can be created at any time, with board approval, to fit the needs of the library. However, any policies created should apply to the majority of patrons and issues, not solve a onetime problem or affect only a few people.

TRAINING

If libraries are institutions of lifelong learning, then all staff in the library should be lifelong learners as well. This means offering staff opportunities for training and learning on a regular basis. Training can be tricky if you have a small budget. Luckily, lots of great free and inexpensive continuing education resources are available. One of the most effective ways to train staff is to have them teach one another. Have someone who is a whiz at Microsoft Excel? Have that person show others how to do different functions in Excel. Having staff train one another provides valuable experience for all parties involved.

Incorporate training into the employee's regular work schedule so it, too, becomes something that is as essential as planning a program, doing collection development, or checking out books.

FEEDBACK AND EVALUATIONS

The new staff member has been hired, onboarded, and trained. Engaged staff members are those who are continually learning and growing, moving themselves, the department, and the library forward. Staff will learn, grow, and have successes and failures. Providing regular feedback to employees during these times is critical. Feedback allows employees to continue to grow and also lets them know where they stand in terms of the work being performed.

When giving feedback, remember to offer both positive and constructive feedback. Giving feedback is an art. Keep in mind these tips when talking to staff:

- Be kind, but realistic.
- Be specific in what is good and what needs improvement.
- Share consequences of what will happen if the behavior doesn't improve.
- Make it about the job they did and not about them personally.
- Make feedback part of regular meetings with staff.
- Don't wait, especially if there is a problem. Give feedback as soon as possible to help the staffer get back on track.

Having regular one-on-one meetings with direct reports makes it easy to have a set place to give feedback. Meeting to touch base will also help employees stay engaged. If feedback becomes part of the normal discussion about projects and work, employees will find it easier to hear when an issue does come up.

In addition to giving regular feedback throughout the year, conduct an annual evaluation that summarizes everything that has been discussed throughout the year. This helps the employee see everything in one place and gain a better understanding of how the employee is doing overall. While annual evaluations are becoming less popular,[2] they still offer a great opportunity to highlight strengths and accomplishments for staff.

DISCIPLINE

A staff member can be onboarded well, thoroughly trained in his or her position, and given feedback on a continual basis but still may not be performing at the level expected or have some behavior issues. The time may come for reprimands or discipline. Directors and managers normally find disciplining employees challenging and may delay doing so until the issue has gotten out of control. This can make managers and other staff miserable and have dire consequences for the overall morale of the library environment.

When disciplining an employee, a best practice is to proceed with a progressive discipline approach. This approach should be outlined in the employee policy manual so that all employees are aware of it. If an employee's work performance or product is lacking, it is in the employee's (and the library's) best interest to have the matter addressed quickly so that corrections can be made. There are times when immediate action may be necessary, but usually warnings and write-ups are sufficient.

Call the employee into a room and have the employee's manager (or another manager or key employee) in the room, if possible. Discuss the issue and listen to the employee's response. Make it clear what you expect from the employee in relation to the employee's position, what the employee is expected to accomplish, how the employee can improve, and what the time frame is. Ask the employee to acknowledge if it is clear what is expected of the employee in the future.

After the first conversation, or warning, regarding the employee's work product or performance, be sure to follow up on the conversation in an e-mail or hard-copy memo. This eliminates any doubt about what was communicated to them verbally, and having the plan in writing clearly outlines future expectations. Often when an employee is brought in for a meeting of this type, the employee doesn't really absorb what is being said. This follow-up written communication will clarify what the employee may (or may not) have heard and also gives more credibility to any future corrective action, up to and including involuntary termination.

If the situation does not improve, it may be necessary to use a formal write-up process or even develop a performance improvement plan (PIP) to outline concrete steps to get the employee performing at the appropriate level. Any such step should

LEGAL EMPLOYMENT LAWS

The legal aspects of human resources can seem daunting to a director, and they can become more complicated if you are dealing with disciplinary issues. Every director should be aware of the laws governing human resources (HR) and what to be on the lookout for. While directors may not be experts in any of these areas, having a basic knowledge of HR is important. If an employee says something regarding an accommodation or uses the words "harassment" or "discrimination," this should signal to you that the comment needs to be taken seriously and you should gather additional information. It may also be necessary to get the library's attorney involved.

Here are some common acronyms and what they stand for:

ACA—Affordable Care Act

ADA—Americans with Disabilities Act

ADEA—Age Discrimination in Employment Act

COBRA—Consolidated Omnibus Budget Reconciliation Act

DOL—Department of Labor

EEOC—Equal Employment Opportunity Commission

EPA—Equal Pay Act

FLSA—Fair Labor Standards Act

FMLA—Family and Medical Leave Act

GINA—Genetic Information Nondiscrimination Act

HIPAA—Health Insurance Portability and Accountability Act

OSHA—Occupational Safety and Health Administration

PDA—Pregnancy Discrimination Act

include a manager and a formal document outlining the issue, describing the previous conversation you had with the employee, and stating the expectations once again. When creating the written document, be concise, including only facts. Emotions and/or opinions have no place in this setting. Be sure to give an appropriate amount of time for the work product to be improved. In the event that the work product or issue does not improve, termination will be the next step. Once the formal write-up is received and reviewed by the employee, have the employee sign the document. The employee doesn't have to agree with what the document contains; the employee must simply acknowledge receipt of the formal write-up. This will also give more credibility to your actions in the event of a termination.

TERMINATION

Termination refers to when any employee leaves the library, whether voluntarily or involuntarily. When someone leaves voluntarily, conduct an exit interview. Ask questions pertaining to onboarding, training, and how the library runs as a whole. Ask the person to discuss any improvements the employee thinks are necessary. This feedback can yield valuable insight into the library and help identify issues of which you are unaware.

Involuntary termination of an employee is one of the most difficult tasks any director, new or seasoned, will ever do. It is never easy knowing that by involuntarily terminating an employee you are removing a source of income from that person. However, you must remember that the employee's actions, behavior, or inability to perform the essential functions of his or her position is the cause of the termination.

An involuntary termination should never take an employee by surprise. If done properly, the employee should already be aware that his or her performance does not meet the standards of the library. Unless there is an egregious incident, the employee should have had multiple conversations with a manager, including written documentation

SAMPLE TERMINATION SCENARIO

An employee has been showing up late to work three to four days a week. Her manager has spoken with her about her tardiness, and Lizzie has promised to do better. She improves for a week after her manager talks to her, but then the pattern begins again. Her manager gives her a verbal and a written warning, but the behavior continues. Her manager speaks with the director, and they determine that the employee needs to be terminated.

They bring her in at the beginning of her shift to meet with the director and manager. Here is what they say:

> We are here today to talk to you about your repeated issues with
> tardiness. Your manager has repeatedly spoken to you about arriving
> on time for your shifts. You have received both a verbal and a written
> warning but continue to consistently arrive late. As a result, we are
> terminating your employment effective immediately. Your manager
> will go with you to your desk to clear out your items. You will receive
> your last paycheck on [date].

The director or manager then gives the employee a termination letter and information on applying for their state's unemployment insurance. (A sample termination checklist is included in part II, "Tools.")

supporting those discussions, regarding his or her performance before the termination. Ideally, at the last discussion, the manager will already have stated that if improvement is not seen, additional actions, up to and including termination, could occur.

When it first becomes apparent that an employee is not performing at the recommended level, it is best to start the documentation process. Documentation is essential for a successful and (hopefully) litigation-free termination. Litigation is always a possibility after an involuntary termination (or even a voluntary termination) for a variety of reasons.

The threat of litigation is never a reason to not terminate someone. Keeping an employee who is not performing is toxic to the workplace, can be a detriment to the library, and can have long-lasting effects. Even if there is no litigation, the employee will likely file for unemployment benefits, and having thorough documentation is necessary to fight the provision of those benefits. The library should have a disciplinary policy or procedure that would outline the process for reprimands and possible termination. (A sample disciplinary policy is included in part II, "Tools.") Strong policies and documentation go a long way when contesting unemployment benefits or facing litigation.

An involuntary termination is often hard on the rest of the staff. When someone is terminated, the rest of the staff may start to worry that they will be next. Sometimes they are happy when someone is let go. Either way, terminating someone can affect the rest of the staff, and you need to be mindful of what you say in the aftermath of a termination.

It is important to be discreet when ending the employment of (or reprimanding) a staff member. In the event of litigation, it is not helpful to have the wrong information circulating. The best practice is to notify staff that the employee is no longer working at the library and that is all that can be said about the issue. The terminated employee may speak to the library staff afterward and may or may not tell them what happened. While the employee can say something about his or her departure, you cannot.

Once hired, staff should constantly be given opportunities to learn and grow, receive feedback on a regular basis, and be evaluated. Good policies and consistency in implementing them will keep the library running smoothly. Addressing issues as they arise and documenting these conversations will help in the event of a termination. A good, knowledgeable staff is necessary for the library to serve its patrons effectively.

✿ REVIEW AND REFLECT

KEY TAKEAWAYS

Hiring an employee means following a set process that includes these steps:

- Writing an effective job description
- Creating a job advertisement

- Following a strong interview process
- Checking candidate references
- Negotiating compensation

An effective job description includes the following:

- Position information
- Job summary
- Qualifications
- Essential job functions
- Working conditions.

After hiring an employee,

- develop an onboarding process,
- consider how to provide ongoing training,
- provide regular feedback, and
- conduct an annual evaluation.

When disciplining or terminating an employee,

- document everything,
- provide training and guidance on performance issues,
- create a timeline for improvement,
- write out a script before talking to the employee, and
- ensure you have provided all legally required documentation (when terminating).

SELF-CHECK

- Who are my employees and how are they paid?
- Where is the personnel policy? Does every staff member have a copy?
- Where are the personnel files stored?
- Do I have a salary schedule? When was it last updated?
- Are there any current personnel situations that I need to be aware of?
- What mechanisms are in place to provide staff with regular feedback?
- Do we do annual evaluations?

QUESTIONS FOR REFLECTION

- How often should I meet with staff?
- What training have managers had on HR topics?
- What training can we offer staff?
- What legal aspects of HR do I need to learn more about?
- Who can I go to if I have HR-related legal questions?

ADDITIONAL RESOURCES

See part II for these additional resources on employees:

- Sample 2.1: New Hire Checklist
- Sample 2.2: Librarian Job Description
- Sample 2.3: Unpaid Leave of Absence Policy
- Sample 2.4: Social Media Policy
- Sample 2.5: Disciplinary Policy
- Sample 2.6: Termination Checklist
- Sample 2.7: Employee Exit Questionnaire

⬇ **Download additional resources on our website at www.librarydirectorstoolkit.com/resources.**

Green, A. *Ask a Manager: How to Navigate Clueless Colleagues, Lunch-Stealing Bosses, and the Rest of Your Life at Work*. New York: Ballantine Books, 2018.

———. *Managing to Change the World: The Nonprofit Manager's Guide to Getting Results*. San Francisco: Jossey-Bass, 2012.

Lencioni, P. *Five Dysfunctions of a Team: Team Assessment*. San Francisco: Pfeiffer, 2012.

Society for Human Resource Management (SHRM). "SHRM—The Voice of All Things Work." https://shrm.org.

Soehner, C., and A. Darling. *Effective Difficult Conversations: A Step-by-Step Guide*. Chicago: ALA Editions, 2017.

NOTES

1. R. Beck and J. Harter, "Why Great Managers Are So Rare," *Business Journal*, March 25, 2014, https://news.gallup.com/businessjournal/167975/why-great-managers-rare.aspx?utmsource=linkwwwv9&utmcampaign=item241955&utmmedium=copy.
2. L. Bodell, "It's Time to Put Performance Reviews on Notice," *Forbes*, April 27, 2018, www.forbes.com/sites/lisabodell/2018/04/27/why-performance-reviews-are-irrelevant-today/#d6bbebd4b63c.

3

TRUSTEES

After reading this chapter, you will know the following:

- What the roles and responsibilities of library trustees are
- How to onboard a new trustee
- What the role of trustees is versus the role of the library director
- How to successfully interact with your trustees

A nother significant component of your job is working with a board of trustees. Most supervisors know what their role is, but with public library trustees, who are appointed or elected by the community, that is not always the case. As the library director, you have as one of your tasks educating your trustees on their role. Ideally, other board members, preferably the board president, can also educate new trustees on their roles and responsibilities, so that they know and adhere to the line between the duties of the director and those of the board. When that line becomes blurred, it can be very difficult for the director to do his or her job effectively.

TRUSTEE RESPONSIBILITIES

What are the board's main responsibilities? They can be broken down into these main categories:

- Financial oversight, including adopting a tax levy and annual budget that meet the financial needs of the library and/or seeking additional funding to ensure the library has sufficient funding
- Hiring a qualified library director and providing ongoing evaluation for the director

- Adopting formal policies that govern the library
- Guiding the library through a strategic planning process that ensures the library has a strategic plan that fits with the library's vision and mission, including an action plan and timeline
- Advocating for the library in the community and with elected officials
- Attending and participating in the board meetings and board committee meetings, if there are any
- Getting involved in library associations, whether local, state, or national

FINANCIAL OVERSIGHT

The board's main function is one of financial oversight. It is the board's duty to ensure that the library has sufficient funding to meet the needs of the patrons. If the library does not have sufficient funding, it will not be able to fulfill the library's core mission to provide programs, materials, and services to the community.

The board is responsible for ensuring the library is appropriately funded, whether it be by passing a levy or soliciting funds. Once the board determines where the funding is coming from, the director constructs a budget that details how the money will be spent. The board approves the budget presented by the director. After approving the budget, the board will monitor the expenditures and revenues by reviewing the monthly financials included in the board members' packets. The financial report should show the following:

1. How much money is available and in what accounts
2. How you are doing on spending based on the budget that was approved
3. What the actual bills are for each vendor, with amounts that the board will then approve

The steps to creating a budget are laid out in chapter 4.

HIRING A QUALIFIED LIBRARY DIRECTOR

One of the other key responsibilities of a board is to hire a qualified library director. Best practices for hiring a qualified director include hiring someone who has a master's degree in library science or similar certification. Depending on the size of the library, its location, and its budget, hiring a degreed director may not always be possible. If the library's situation does not allow for the former, the board should try to find someone who has previous library experience or who has a passion for public service and the willingness and ability to attend training.

A healthy process for a board to follow when seeking to hire a qualified director should include constructing a thorough job description, crafting a strong job advertisement, carefully reviewing applicants, interviewing with preplanned questions, and offering staff an opportunity to provide feedback. Ensuring that the salary is commensurate with the job responsibilities and the applicant's experience is also important. While the board members may choose to do this themselves, they may instead choose to hire a consultant. The consultant would then guide them through the process of hiring a director. A consultant is a good choice if the board can afford to hire one, as a consultant will have processes in place to ensure that the board hires a qualified director in a timely manner.

POLICY ADOPTION

While the board should not be responsible for the day-to-day running of the library, it is responsible for providing the framework for the library to move in the direction it needs to go. One of the ways to provide that framework is through crafting policies. These policies guide the library staff on running the library and give them direction on how to handle various situations. The director crafts the policies and then the board reviews and approves the policies. Boards should provide feedback on presented policies but should not craft policies from scratch. Chapter 6 provides more detail on crafting policies.

STRATEGIC PLAN DEVELOPMENT

Every library should have a mission and vision statement and a strategic plan, which are covered in chapter 11. The board should revisit the strategic plan on a regular basis and make adjustments as needs change. The plan is essential in helping to focus the library's efforts in the future. With so many options for achieving what library staff need and want to accomplish for the community, having a clear focus is essential for the board, the director, and the staff.

ADVOCACY

While a board member may not act on his or her own because the board can take action only as a whole, an individual board member can and should be an advocate for the library at a local level. Following are some examples of local advocacy:

- Attend community events and help share information at a library table.
- Participate in a service organization like Lions, Kiwanis, or Rotary and use it as a forum to educate others about the library.
- Talk to family, friends, and neighbors about what new things the library is doing and share upcoming programs and events.

- Stay in tune with the other local municipalities and their elected officials so they know what is happening with the schools, village/city, or park districts.

Board members can also advocate at the state or federal level. This involves getting in touch with local elected officials and advocating for either your library or for the library community in general. Following are examples of state or federal advocacy:

- Call legislators regularly to tell them what is going on at the library.
- Stay informed about laws impacting libraries (as the director it is your job to keep the board apprised of any pressing laws or potential legislation).
- Attend legislative meet-and-greets when offered; these are excellent opportunities to learn about what is going on legislatively and for meeting elected officials from outside your library area.
- Participate in National Library Legislative Day, which happens each May in Washington, DC, or online.

GETTING INVOLVED

In addition to advocating for the library, board members should also be encouraged to get involved in regional, state, and national library associations and groups. Starting at

TALKING TO LEGISLATORS

Talking to legislators can be intimidating, whether you are a board member or the library director. Here are some tips to help make it a little easier.

- Build a relationship with your legislators and their staff.
- Accept that you will not always get to talk to the legislator. Creating a relationship with the chief of staff or assistants is a great way to get a legislator's ear.
- Talk to legislators regularly about your library and what you are doing for the community. Don't wait until you have an issue to speak to them.
- Legislators are busy and their time is limited. Be clear about why you are calling and have all your information available to give (or e-mail) when asked.
- Assume the legislators know nothing about your library.
- Share your successes so the legislators are hearing positive things.
- Make sure the legislators are getting your marketing pieces, like your newsletter, Facebook posts, or other social media feeds.
- Above all, remember that legislators are people, too, and don't bombard them or attack them over a perceived injustice.

the top is the American Library Association, which has an entire arm for library trustees called Association for Library Trustees and Advocates (ALTA). Most states have state library associations, and many also have regional ones.

These organizations offer information, classes and workshops, and networking opportunities so your trustees can get involved and meet other trustees. While technically not an official requirement for trustees, a trustee who participates in advocacy at any level is more likely to be an engaged board member and a strong, supportive trustee.

TRUSTEE ORIENTATION

When a new trustee joins the board, whether through an election or appointment, having a plan for the trustee's orientation is critical to helping the trustee become acclimated to the library and other board members. The orientation sets the stage for what you can expect from a board member in the future and gives you an opportunity to align the new trustee with your philosophies.

After the election or appointment, call the trustee to welcome that person to the board and to explain how much you are looking forward to working with the trustee. Follow up with a welcome letter that includes some basic information. See part II, "Tools," for a trustee welcome letter.

After you welcome your new trustee, schedule an orientation. Provide each new board member with a binder or digital copies of important information. Here is a sample of what you can include in the binder:

1. General library information
    a. Contact information
    b. Mission statement
    c. Organizational chart
2. Board of trustees' names and phone numbers
3. Key staff contact information
4. Calendars
    a. Board meeting dates
    b. Holiday schedule
    c. Annual calendar of actions to be taken at board meetings
5. Director's reports (past six months)
6. Minutes (past six months)
7. Financial reports (past six months)
8. Annual library budget
9. Board bylaws
10. General library policies
11. Any other large-scale projects (master plans, capital improvement plans, etc.)
12. Additional resources from your local library system or association

SAMPLE BOARD MEMBER ORIENTATION AGENDA

Creating an agenda for the actual meeting helps you stay on track and cover all the salient details. Here is a sample agenda:

1. Welcome
2. Duties and role of the board versus duties and role of the director
3. Library structures in your state
   a. Your state library
   b. Library system (if applicable)
   c. Funding and your state libraries
4. Important policies and laws
   a. State laws (varies by state)
   b. Personnel
   c. Unattended children
   d. Circulation
   e. Bylaws
5. Budget
   a. Review of prior month's treasurer's report
   b. Review of different reserve accounts
6. Library tour
7. Strategic plan review

The orientation usually takes about two to three hours. The trustee should leave with a good knowledge of how the library runs, how the board meetings run, and any projects that the library is currently working on. This will help bring the new trustee up to speed at his or her first meeting.

CONTINUING EDUCATION

When a new trustee comes on board, offer the trustee opportunities to attend continuing education. Most states or library systems offer regular training following local elections and often provide training during other times of the year. Other avenues for training trustees include the webinars available on ALA's United for Libraries webpage and WebJunction's "Friends, Trustees and Volunteers." Sending trustees to observe other board meetings (e.g., of the village/city or the local school boards) is a great way for them to observe parliamentary procedure in action. New trustees aren't the only ones who need continuing education; all board members should take advantage of these opportunities. The new trustee orientation is also a great way to train other board members. Invite the entire board to all or part of the orientation as a refresher course.

During the next year, when an annual agenda item (e.g., the levy) comes up, touch base with the new board member before the meeting and give the new trustee a little more detail on that topic. Take time during the meeting to go over regularly recurring items in more depth. Encourage the trustee to call you with questions. There is a lot of information for a new trustee to learn and helping the new trustee learn will make that trustee a better board member. Be proactive in your training of the new trustee; doing so will give you a greater chance of having an engaged and informed board member.

BOARD MEETINGS

Most libraries have at least one monthly board meeting to take care of library business. The library may also have additional meetings throughout the month, in addition to the regular board meeting, depending on the specific library's needs. These additional meetings can be special meetings, committee meetings, committee of the whole meetings, or some other combination.

You should prepare a packet for each board meeting that includes an agenda, minutes from the previous meeting, monthly financial information (including receipts and expenditures), and any supporting documentation for what is on the agenda. Copies of this packet may be given to your board members in a variety of ways. They can be printed and dropped off in person or mailed to their residences, or they can be submitted in an electronic format for them to retrieve online. No matter the delivery method, these documents must be given to the board members for their review in advance of the board meeting. Best practice is to send out packets a week prior to the meeting so the board has sufficient time to review the information. Some states have very specific rules about when a public board is to receive board packets. Check your state statutes to ensure you are complying with the law.

Each state differs on retention policies for local records, but board minutes, treasurer's reports, and board packets must typically be retained for a longer period of time or indefinitely. Check your local record retention policies to see what you need to keep and for how long. Retention policies also address e-mail communications, and board members' e-mails are usually considered part of the public record. E-mail communications between board members may be allowed, depending on your local laws, but you should check the rules and make sure your board members are aware of those rules. Illinois, for example, has fairly strong rules and regulations surrounding communication between board members outside of meetings and requires new trustees to take a training course on the Open Meetings Act.

If reading the board packet is the first responsibility of a board member, meeting attendance is the second. The business of the library can take place only when the board approves finances, strategic plans, policies, and so forth, and can be accomplished only if enough board members attend the meetings on a regular basis. Regular attendance at meetings will also ensure that board members are kept abreast of all the major decisions that are happening at the library and are privy to the conversations that helped shape those decisions. Board minutes are great to have for reference, but they are a record of only the nuts-and-bolts of the meeting and normally do not cover discussion in great detail.

Many states have minimum meeting requirements for public entities. It may (or may not) be possible to remove a trustee for nonattendance. Check with your state's statutes for further information.

In addition to the regular monthly meetings, many library boards have committees as well. Committees come in many different shapes and sizes, and their role as part of your board is laid out in the board bylaws, which dictate how the board operates. Some boards may have standing committees on topics such as these:

- Finance
- Policy and bylaws
- Buildings and grounds
- Personnel
- Strategic plan
- Development and fund-raising

Standing committees may meet monthly, quarterly, or only when needed. Instead of standing committee meetings, some boards prefer to have meetings of the whole for specific topics, for example, an annual budget meeting or quarterly policy meetings. Each board and library will be unique, so you need to find out what approach your board prefers. Read previous board packets to determine what committees your board typically has and how frequently they meet and to get a sense of the type of information presented.

Committee work has its pros and cons. For instance, when crafting new policies, preparing a budget, or addressing facility issues, a committee may look at a first draft or do some brainstorming. A committee can be a good place to work out issues or develop solutions to problems before bringing the topic to the full board. However, at times, the full board may choose to redo all the previous work done by a committee. Another downside to committees is the extra time required for the board to meet. As board members are volunteers, having a large number of committee meetings they must attend places an extra burden on their shoulders. In addition, the director must create agendas and packets, ensure the meetings are properly posted, and handle the minutes from all of these committee meetings.

Depending on how effective your committees are, expending this extra effort may not be a good use of your time. There is no right or wrong answer when it comes to forming board committees. Boards and directors will change, and evaluating committees as the principals change will help your board remain relevant to all your board members.

THE BOARD-DIRECTOR RELATIONSHIP

One of the most difficult parts of being a director is defining the role of the board versus the role of the director for your library board. Check out part II, "Tools," for a chart of board and director responsibilities. The key thing to remember is that the board has only one employee: you. You are in charge of all the other employees at the library.

The library director should be the main point of contact for the board and is responsible for preparing the board packets, answering questions from the board, and training the board members on their roles and responsibilities. In addition to being an informational advisor about the work of the library, the director needs to foster positive relationships with board members individually and with the board as a whole.

Board–director relationships can be frustrating, challenging, rewarding, and sometimes even easy. Even if you have a good or great board, you may still run into differences of opinion from time to time. What is important to remember is that a board acts as a whole; no one on the board has the authority to act independently. They must act in concert on decision making.

To foster positive relationships between you and the board, you need to understand where your trustees are coming from. Why do they want to be on the board? What is their background? What are their passions? Once you have a clearer understanding of board members, consider their viewpoints when presenting different topics and issues. Ask what they are hearing about the library in the community and listen closely to their responses. Make sure you are providing them with solid information to make informed decisions. Strong communication is key to fostering a positive relationship between you and your board. We recommend meeting one-on-one with each board member to get a sense of where they are coming from. Meeting with the large group can be beneficial, too, but will have a different dynamic than is found in one-on-one conversations.

There may be times when board members overstep the line between board and director. The board members may not understand that the board acts as a whole and that no one board member has any individual power. This situation can be difficult to navigate. The strongest library director would have a hard time managing such board members. You want to cultivate good relationships, so it behooves you to respond when board members ask questions. If a board member is being overly persistent, make sure you understand where that person is coming from, what the person's background is, and why this person is on the board. If the situation becomes problematic, talk to your board president or take the issue to your library system or state library—ask for help.

What about when you have an entire board that is behaving badly or possibly breaking the law? Sadly, this happens, and it can be very difficult to handle. Your board supervises you and has the ability to discipline you or terminate your employment. You should have a whistleblower policy in your personnel manual that will protect you in the event that your board is doing something illegal and you call them out on it. When handling issues with boards, you should be respectful and call in outside help as needed.

Contact your neighboring library directors and ask for advice. Someone may have had a similar situation and can guide you. You can also seek help from a more official source. There are outside consultants that offer library board training; these consultants can come in and speak with the board or offer alternative options for board training. Your library attorney is also a good source of information and support. Your state library or library system will also often have support systems in place for these situations. The trustee division of ALA, United for Libraries, also offers a wide variety of training materials. The best thing you can do is work on establishing a good rapport with your board and be proactive in fostering your relationship with them. But if you can't avoid a board behaving badly, know that there is help out there. You are not alone.

✿ REVIEW AND REFLECT

KEY TAKEAWAYS

Trustees are responsible for

- ensuring the library is appropriately funded,
- hiring and evaluating a qualified library director,
- adopting policies to govern the library,
- developing a strategic plan,
- advocating for the library and talking to legislators, and
- representing the library in the community.

When new trustees join the board, offer an orientation process that includes reviewing

- board member responsibilities,
- the library budget,
- library laws, and
- library projects.

Board packets are composed of the following:

- Agenda
- Minutes from previous meeting
- Financial statement
- Director's report
- Supporting documentation for agenda items
- Statistics

The board–director relationship is important, and directors should take the opportunity to build relationships with the board as a whole and with board members as individuals.

SELF-CHECK

- When and where are board meetings held?
- How is the board packet assembled and distributed?
- Do I know where my board bylaws are and have I read them?
- Is there a timeline for key board decisions each year?
- Do I have a calendar of important legal dates for board meetings?

QUESTIONS FOR REFLECTION

- What kind of relationship do I currently have with my board?
- What kind of relationship would I like to have with my board?
- What are the backgrounds of my board members? How do their backgrounds affect their view of the library?
- Do I understand what my responsibilities are as a library director?
- Have I developed a communication strategy with my board?

ADDITIONAL RESOURCES

See part II for these additional resources for working with trustees:

- Sample 3.1: Trustee Welcome Letter
- Sample 3.2: Library Board versus Director Role

Moore, M. Y. *The Successful Library Trustee Handbook*. Chicago: American Library Association, 2010.

Reed, S. G., and J. Kalonick. *The Complete Library Trustee Handbook*. New York: Neal-Schuman, 2010.

United for Libraries. Website of the Association of Library Trustees, Advocates, Friends and Foundations, a division of the American Library Association. www.ala.org/united.

WebJunction. "Friends, Trustees and Volunteers." www.webjunction.org/explore-topics/friends-trustees.html.

4

FINANCES

After reading this chapter, you will know the following:

- ■ Where library revenue comes from
- ■ How to determine spending and create a budget
- ■ The role of the board in approving and implementing a budget
- ■ What needs to happen with monthly and annual finance reviews

H ow a budget is crafted sets the stage for how the library will run. The budget determines where to focus your energies over the next year by allocating funding to the areas that require the most focus. Understanding where the library funding comes from and how it is expended is important in ensuring a financially stable library. A budget includes revenues and expenditures. While the library director and staff do the work of crafting the budget, the board plays a critical role in approving the budget and monitoring the ongoing expenditures. When well crafted, the budget becomes a tool that the library director and board will use as a guide throughout the year.

REVENUES

Where does the library's money come from? Many libraries receive the majority of their funding from local or municipal funding.[1] While every library is different and different states have different funding models, this section discusses a typical breakdown for Illinois libraries and provides an example budget in table 4.1.

TAXES

Property taxes usually make up the majority of a library's revenue, but other types of taxes can also be included. In Illinois, many libraries receive personal property

TABLE 4.1 Revenues Budget Table

REVENUE	FY 2020 BUDGET ($)	% OF OVERALL BUDGET
Taxes	**Target**	**97.0**
Property taxes	676,000	90.1
Other taxes	23,000	3.1
Interest income	1,000	0.1
	700,000	**93.3**
Federal/State	**Target**	**1.0**
Other	1,000	0.1
Fines and Fees	**Target**	**1.0**
Lost/damaged items	1,800	0.2
Nonresident fees	2,000	0.3
Overdue fines	10,200	1.4
Printing and copying	5,500	0.7
	19,500	**2.6**
Grants	**Target**	**0.5**
General	5,000	0.7
State library grants	14,000	1.9
	19,000	**2.6**
Foundation or Friends	**Target**	**0.5**
Endowment	4,500	0.6
Book sales	3,000	0.4
	7,500	**1.0**
Donations	**3,000**	**0.4**
TOTAL REVENUE	**750,000**	**100.0**

replacement tax and some libraries receive sales tax from their local municipalities, county, or state.

FEDERAL OR STATE FUNDING

Depending on their state, libraries may receive regular, sustainable funding or it may be more project or need based. Federal funds come from the LSTA (Library Services and Technology Act) and E-rate (Universal Service Program for Schools and Libraries) and may flow directly to the library or through the state.

FINES AND FEES

This revenue category includes fines for overdue and lost books, copier and printing fees, as well as things like rental fees. Examples of such fees include meeting room rentals or equipment rentals. For example, a library might rent out its meeting room and charge a fee to use the room or not charge to use the room but charge for the use of equipment in the room.

GRANTS

Grants are often a way to supplement the library's budget. Some grants have a simple application process and can be applied for annually, which means they can be used as a regular source of income, while others may be a one-time grant to fund a special project. Depending on the state laws for your budgeting process, you may want to keep a grant line in your budget and allocate some money in that line, even if you don't expect to apply for or receive a grant. In some states, you will not be able to expend funds if you have not delineated those funds in a budget line.

FOUNDATIONS AND FRIENDS OF THE LIBRARY

Foundations and Friends of the Library are separate organizations from the library, though their mission is to fund-raise for the needs of the library. If these groups supply a consistent source of funding, consider making them a separate budget line. The library director will typically have a close relationship with a Foundation or Friends of the Library group, and being able to track the funding more closely can be helpful in ensuring you recognize these groups for their efforts.

DONATIONS, BEQUESTS, AND ENDOWMENTS

In addition to donations made in honor of someone, the library may also receive bequests, which are donations left to the library in someone's will. Some libraries receive an annual revenue stream called an endowment, which is typically from a group or organization that has invested funds that accrue interest. The monies from the interest are given to the library on an annual basis to supplement the expenses of the library. An endowment may specify how the monies from the endowment may be spent, such as on collections or programming, so a library will need to determine if it wants to accept the terms of the endowment before receiving the monies. A library might also get larger donations for capital projects, which would increase this category's percentage of the budget.

EXPENSES

In order to successfully run the library, you need to have in place a solid plan about how the money will be spent in the library. The operating budget serves as a road map for

BUDGET TERMS TO KNOW

Assessed property value: This is the amount each property in your taxing area is worth. It is used to calculate how much money you will receive in taxes.

Capital fund: This is the money that you set aside to use for large building and technology improvements. In most states, once these funds are designated for this purpose, they cannot be used for any other purpose.

Debt service: This refers to the money owed to the lending source after borrowing funds for a major capital improvement project, usually a new or renovated building. This money can typically be spent only on repaying the debt you have incurred and needs to be in a separate budget line.

Developer (impact) fees: In some states, these are the fees received from developers after they have built new residences but before anyone moves in and starts paying taxes. This covers the time in between and is received either once the structure is built or not until someone has moved in.

Expenditures: This refers to the money that is being spent by the library.

Fiscal year: Your fiscal year is the twelve-month period your library uses for accounting and auditing purposes, which is determined by the type of library.

Fund balance: Your fund balance is your assets minus your liabilities.

Operating budget: This budget tells you where to spend your money based on how much you are bringing in for your fiscal year.

Reserve fund: These are the funds you have set aside for future projects or needs. Your capital fund is part of your overall reserve fund.

Revenue: This refers to the money that your library receives.

how monies are to be spent over the next fiscal year. This section discusses some general categories that, no matter the size of your budget, should be included in the operating budget and provides an example budget in table 4.2.

PERSONNEL

This should be the largest percentage of your budget and is generally 50 to 80 percent of expenditures.[2] Included in the personnel category are salaries, benefits (including pensions), FICA (Federal Insurance Contributions Act; aka Social Security), health insurance, and life insurance.

COLLECTIONS

This expense category covers all the materials purchased for the library, including print materials, audiovisual items, e-books, and databases and typically accounts for 8 to 20 percent of the budget.[3] Other expenses in this line item include technical services processing costs, shipping from book vendors, consortium fees, or ILS (integrated library system) costs. Library budgeting formats will be different and may have expenses in different categories based on the library's past practices, legal requirements, and what seems logical to you.

FACILITIES

Library facilities need to be maintained, and a budget must be set to provide for items like toilet paper, cleaning supplies, and the like. Other building costs include annual inspections, equipment maintenance, contracts with outside vendors for HVAC (heating, ventilation, and air conditioning) maintenance, snow removal, landscaping, janitorial services, and anything else necessary for the maintenance of the building and grounds. Utility costs may be included in this line.

INSURANCE

Chapter 7 covers different types of insurance in depth, but they generally fall into a few basic categories:

- Health, which covers medical, dental, and sometimes life insurance
- Building, which includes liability insurance for directors and officers, cyber security, flooding, and so forth
- Personnel, which includes workers' compensation and unemployment insurance

Most years, these costs will go up a little bit. Check with the library's insurance provider to inquire about potential increases each year.

TABLE 4.2 Expenses Budget Table

EXPENSES	FY 2020 BUDGET ($)	% OF OVERALL BUDGET
Personnel		
Salaries and wages	375,000	50.0
Pension	48,000	6.4
Group insurance	30,000	4.0
Social Security	30,900	4.1
	483,900	**64.5**
Collections		
Books	50,000	6.7
E-books	10,000	1.3
Periodicals	5,000	0.7
Databases	7,000	0.9
Media	7,000	0.9
Audiobooks	5,000	0.7
	84,000	**11.2**
Facilities		
Building maintenance	40,000	5.3
Utilities	20,000	2.7
Janitorial supplies	1,000	0.1
	61,000	**8.1**
Insurance		
Unemployment	1,000	0.1
Property insurance	5,500	0.7
Workers' compensation	2,500	0.3
Liability insurance	6,000	0.8
	15,000	**1.9**
Programming		

EXPENSES	FY 2020 BUDGET ($)	% OF OVERALL BUDGET
Programming	9,000	1.2
Professional Development		
Professional development	5,000	0.7
Contractual Services		
Legal	3,500	0.5
Payroll	4,000	0.5
Integrated library system	16,000	2.1
Collection agency	600	0.1
Consulting fees	1,000	0.1
Audit	3,000	0.4
	28,100	**3.7**
Other		
Office supplies	4,500	0.6
Internet/phone	4,500	0.6
Postage	1,500	0.2
Copy machines	5,000	0.7
Hardware/software	5,000	0.7
Marketing/public relations	5,000	0.7
Furniture/fixtures	2,000	0.3
Equipment	1,000	0.1
Contingencies	35,500	4.7
	64,000	**8.6**
TOTAL EXPENSES	**750,000**	**100.0**

ADDITIONAL EXPENSE LINE ITEMS

After the core fiscal needs of the library are covered, additional lines can be added. These line items will vary from library to library. The most common line items are these:

- *Programming:* Depending on the size of your library, you may break this down by age or department (e.g., youth, adult) or type of program or it may be just one line. This line may include performers, supplies, and any other programming-related costs as well as funds for reading clubs and other larger initiatives.
- *Marketing/public relations (PR):* To remain relevant, a library will need to market itself to the community. This line can include any outreach costs, ads, print or electronic newsletters, postage to pay for mailings, and any other marketing costs associated with informing the public about library events.
- *Staff/trustee development:* This line includes funding for all continuing education–related expenses for staff and board members, such as classes (including travel expenses to get there and back), relevant conferences or training (with food, lodging, and travel included), and professional memberships.
- *Contractual accounts:* The library often employs outside consultants for certain work. The most obvious consultant is the library attorney. The attorney can review policies and contracts, help with personnel issues, and so on. Be sure to allocate enough funds to cover this work. Other outside consultants or vendors may be needed for the library audit or IT services. Review prior years' budgets to see where monies have been spent in the past to determine how to allocate funds for the future.

Other types of expenses may include general library and office supplies, furniture, and equipment. It is also a good practice to have a contingency line item to provide for small unexpected expenses.

BUDGET PROCESS

Now that the general components of the budget are in place, let's examine where the money comes from and how it is all put together. There are many formal methods that you can use to assemble your budget, including these:

- Line-by-line budgeting
- Formula budgeting
- Program budgeting
- Performance budgeting

- Planning-programming-budgeting system (PPBS)
- Zero-based budgeting

However, we have found it most effective to take a little from each of these types of budgeting method to prepare your budget. We do not discuss each of these categories in depth here but instead recommend that you read *Financial Management for Libraries* by William Sannwald.

GATHER THE DATA

Start by gathering the numbers for each budget line from the previous few years to evaluate the spending trends. Look at the current year and project how much you anticipate spending by the end of the fiscal year by looking at the budget and evaluating what your monthly, quarterly, and annual costs have been thus far. Determine where your spending is at for the year and project where you anticipate ending up at the end of the year. Table 4.3 presents an example of what that might look like.

When reviewing the budget, look at trends over several years of spending. Put three or four previous fiscal years on the spreadsheet so you can see how the lines change over time. Make a note of any budget lines that are over or under. Why did this happen? Oftentimes it is because of a one-time emergency or opportunity or occurrence. Determine how these line items need to be adjusted to ensure that money isn't being allocated incorrectly. Make sure to note the reason for these changes on the budget worksheet to memorialize for the next year's budget work. A sample budget and budget template are included in part II, "Tools."

Once you have completed an evaluation of the previous year's data, gather the information for all categories necessary to keep the library open. This will include the following:

TABLE 4.3 Budget Preparation Table

	ANNUAL	MONTHLY
Budget	$10,000	$833 ($10,000/12 months)
Expenditures 8 Months In	$5,000	$625 ($5,000/8 months)
Expected Remaining Expenditures	$2,500 ($625 × 4)	$625 (average spending)
Anticipated Total Spent (by End of Fiscal Year)	$7,500	$625
Percentage of Budget Spent	75%	

- Staff (payroll)
- Insurance (health, workers' compensation, building, etc.)
- Utilities (electric, gas, phone, and Internet)
- Maintenance costs (annual inspections, repairs, etc.)

Health insurance, liability insurance, and database vendors will need to be contacted to ascertain the coming year's approximate increases. The easiest way to keep track of this is to maintain a contract database for all outside vendors and then contact them during the budgeting process. A contract database is available on our website (www.library-directorstoolkit.com/resources).

Involving staff in the budgeting process is important to ensure that everything will be captured during the budget process for the coming year. Provide appropriate staff, usually the management team, with copies of the budget worksheets so they can see what previous years' budgets have looked like. Ask them to provide projected numbers on how much they would like to spend in the following areas:

- Databases
- Downloadables
- Physical collections
- Programming
- Marketing
- Furniture and equipment (often a wish list until other numbers are finalized)
- Other requests

Give staff two to four weeks to complete the worksheets. If staff have not been involved in the budgeting process previously, you should spend more time working with and explaining the different lines to them. Be sure to remind the staff that the numbers they submit are requests only and nothing is finalized until you review all the budget numbers and submit the budget to the board for final approval.

While completing the previous tasks, gather information on projects that will be undertaken in the coming year. When determining what to gather, look at the following:

- *Strategic plan:* What is included in the plans for the coming year?
- *Technology replacement plan:* What equipment needs to be replaced?
- *Capital improvement plan:* What building systems need to be updated? Landscaping? Furniture? Building remodel/renovation?
- *Projects:* What projects have been identified to be completed in the next year? What projects has the board identified for the library to focus on in the next year?
- *Community projects:* Are there any community-wide projects that the library wants/needs to take part in, such as a new bike path, community garden, and so on?

CRUNCH THE NUMBERS

Once all the numbers are gathered, the revenue and expenditure data can be entered into a spreadsheet. Personnel is typically the largest budget line, so put the expected staffing and benefits costs in first. Input all other known costs: health and liability insurance; utilities; collection costs, including database contracts; any other contractual agreements; and projected facility maintenance costs for the next year. Be sure to include any special line items like bond payments, mortgages, or loans, such as tax anticipation warrants.

Next, input the variable costs like materials, programming, professional development, and so forth. Sometimes it might be difficult to know which line item something falls in; put it where it makes sense and keep a list of line item account numbers and what goes into each account. This comes in handy when coding future invoices and training new managers and trustees.

Once all the numbers have been entered, review the totals at the bottom. Is the budget in the red or the black? If it is in the red, there is more going out than coming in and the numbers will have to be readjusted. This can be a difficult task involving the evaluation and prioritization of certain lines. The lines must, at minimum, meet the revenue coming in. This prioritization may take a few tries to get the budget lines to balance and may result in extra requests being removed from the budget.

The latter items are now wish list items for future funding options. Keep them handy so if a potential donor contacts the library with a desire to donate money, you will have a list of ideas for purchases at the ready. Share the list with staff so they are aware of what was and wasn't included in the budget, and so they are ready for allocating funding if the opportunity arises.

REVIEW, REVIEW, REVIEW

Once you have created a draft budget, have a manager or bookkeeper review it. If instead someone else puts the numbers together for you, you should review the draft. During the review process, if you make a change in a line, be sure to note why so you remember for future years. Review and tweak the numbers, asking for input from others when needed, until the budget is ready to present to the board.

LOOK TO THE FUTURE

Once the general operating budget is organized, consider any larger projects that are necessary for the library. These projects are generally paid for from a capital improvement budget fund or reserve fund, which are separate from the operating budget. Projects might include building renovations, new buildings, IT upgrades, or larger maintenance projects, like painting or lighting upgrades. The list of capital projects should be presented to the board when the rest of the budget is ready, but as a separate budget from the general operating one.

Often these projects can be quite expensive, so you will need a plan for saving money to and expending money from the special accounts. Each state differs in how reserve funds work for such projects and how funds can be set aside to pay for them. Look to your state's statutes to determine the amount of funds allowed to be set aside for special projects and the process for doing so.

If all goes well, there may be funds remaining at the end of the fiscal year. Your library should adopt a financial policy that details how much is to be kept in reserve in the general fund and how much is to be transferred to special funds annually.

GAIN BOARD APPROVAL

Now that a budget has been created, you may be wondering what the role of the board is in the budgeting process. The board does not create the budget; the library director puts the numbers together to present to the board. The board is responsible for approving the budget and may make some suggestions that may impact some of the line items, such as staff salaries/raises. The budget may get changed based on the board's feedback, but board members should not be doing the actual budget preparation and number crunching.

Some boards may have a finance committee, and the library director will work with the treasurer and other board members to come up with the draft budget. Best practice recommends the entire board review the draft budget at a regular board meeting or a special meeting of the whole. Budget approval is a critical task for the board, and it is wise to make sure the full board is aware of how much funding the library receives and how much will be expended annually.

The approval process usually takes two months. During the first month, after the library director has presented the draft budget to the full board, the library director goes over the budget, line by line if necessary. Trustees usually take this time to ask questions and provide feedback. The library director takes that feedback, reworks some of the line items, and presents the revised budget for final approval the following month. Sometimes this process can be done with one board meeting; however, if suggestions are made, it may be difficult to incorporate those changes at the meeting and update the document immediately. Spreading the process over two meetings enables the board and director to think about the budget as presented and perhaps catch something that may have been missed.

When presenting the budget, how much information should you provide? Every library has a different budget style and budgeting procedures. How you present a budget to your board will be based on the level of detail your board members want to see in their budget documents. At minimum, the board should get a general overview, with no need to provide a breakdown of every single category unless that is specifically requested.

Board members may want more information in certain areas, and you should ensure they have the information they need to make an informed decision. Depending on the background of each board member and the past practices of presenting the budget, you may have to explain more or less. Use a notes field in your spreadsheet to record any items that are not part of the regular expenditures, such as staff raises or new equipment. Ask the board how the budget was presented in prior years or look at previous years' board packets to help get a sense of how much information is usually included.

THE BUDGET DAY TO DAY

After the board approves the budget, share the final budget with the appropriate staff so they can plan their departmental budgets for the coming year. How this information will be shared with staff will depend on the number of staff involved. If the library has a large staff, the director may want to sit down with all the managers and go through the budget lines, highlighting each department. In a smaller library, the director might give the staff the overall budget and hold an informal conversation. The more informed library staff members are regarding the budget, the better prepared they will be to spend money wisely. When presenting to staff, be sure to follow up on requests that they have made and alert them as to whether those items are officially in the budget or not. Let staff members know about any large projects taking place based on the approved budget so they are aware of the priorities for the year.

Once the new fiscal year starts, one of the main roles of the director is to keep track of the budget. Depending on the size of your library, you may have a bookkeeper on staff to help with this task.

Each month, gather all invoices received and verify that the invoices correlate with received services or products. Once you have gathered the invoices, you should review and initial them. If using a bookkeeper, that person may do part of this, but you should sign off on each invoice. Confirm that there are no extra charges and that everything ordered has been received before approving for payment. If your library has a petty cash account, you will need to reconcile this account monthly and submit that information along with the monthly bills for board approval.

The library bank accounts need to be reviewed and reconciled by using the monthly bank statements to ensure that all monies allocated for bills and payroll for the prior month have been withdrawn by the vendors. This information is used to create the library's monthly financial statement. If you are unsure of the best method for reviewing all the library's accounts and don't have a business manager, bookkeeper, or an outside firm that helps with the accounting, contact your auditor for advice. There are also accounting software packages, like QuickBooks, available for purchase that will help you organize the library's finances.

Once the invoices and bank statements have been reviewed and reconciled, you should create a monthly financial report for presentation to the board. At minimum, the report should include the following:

- How much money is in each library bank account
- How much revenue has been received by the library to date for that fiscal year and how much more is expected to be received for the remainder of the fiscal year
- How much has been spent in each line item of the approved budget and how much is left in each line item for the remainder of the year

A record of the current month's invoices listing the name of the payee company, a general description of what was bought, the budget line, and the amount due should be included in the board packet every month for board approval.

Many libraries post their treasurer's reports or monthly financials on their websites, and these provide good examples of the different possible formats that you can use. Each library grows accustomed to a specific type of report. Discuss with your board members what they prefer to see report-wise. If they don't want to read or can't understand the report you create, they will not be able to make informed decisions.

ANNUAL AUDIT

Depending on the statutes of your state and the size of your budget, it may not be legally required for your library to do an annual audit. However, even if an audit is not legally required, it is a best practice to have an external entity review your books and check your accounting practices, especially since you are handling public funds.

After the fiscal year concludes and the books are closed out for the year, the library auditor will come in and review all financial transactions for the prior fiscal year. The auditor is not only reviewing the year but also making sure that the numbers were input correctly and that there are no issues with the internal processes for handling funds. The auditor will look at bank statements and specific bills and ask about how the library director/bookkeeper/treasurer reviews them and what the process is for accounting for the cash taken in. The auditor will review the monthly reports and may even want to ask the board some questions.

Once the auditor has gathered all the necessary data, the auditor will prepare the audit, following the generally accepted accounting principles developed by the Governmental Accounting Standards Board (GASB) to assess the information the auditor has received. Once the audit is complete, the auditor should review the audit with the library director. An audit looks very different from the monthly financials and takes into account a larger view of the financial health of the library. Be sure to ask the auditor as many questions as necessary for you to have a full understanding of the audit document.

After completion, the audit should be presented to the board for their acceptance. Board members do not approve the audit, as they are not making a judgment on what the auditor has prepared, but they do need to accept it so that it becomes part of the official documents of the library. It is not uncommon for the auditor to come to the board meeting and present the audit to the board.

The audit is the final piece in your yearlong work with the budget. Now it is time to start all over again.

✿ REVIEW AND REFLECT

KEY TAKEAWAYS

Library revenues typically fall into these categories:

- Taxes
- Federal or state funding
- Fines and fees
- Grants
- Foundations and Friends of the Library donations, bequests, and endowments

Expenses can be broken down into these main categories:

- Personnel
- Collections
- Facilities
- Insurance
- Other

When creating a budget, follow a set process:

- Gather the data.
- Crunch the numbers.
- Review, review, review.
- Look to the future.
- Gain board approval.

Using the budget day to day means

- preparing monthly reports for the board,
- reviewing invoices and bank records, and
- monitoring budget lines.

While not always required, an annual audit is a good idea, as is having an outside financial professional review the library's financials.

SELF-CHECK

- Where is my library's budget?
- How involved is the board in the budgeting process at my library?
- Who handles the day-to-day accounting at my library?
- What does the monthly treasurer's report look like?
- Who handles putting together the monthly report and what information is shared?
- What other information do we provide for the board?
- What information do staff members receive on the budget and monthly expenditures?
- Who does our annual audit?
- Where are previous audits located? Have I read through them?

QUESTIONS FOR REFLECTION

- What type of budget process do I want to have for my library?
- What level of involvement should staff have in the budgeting process?
- What level of involvement should the board have?
- What is the timeline for my budget process, including board review and approval?
- What practices do I need to put in place to ensure the budgeted funds are spent responsibly?
- What internal controls do I need to set up so that we have good checks and balances in our accounting processes?

ADDITIONAL RESOURCES

See part II for these additional resources on finances:

- Sample 4.1: Revenues Budget Template
- Sample 4.2: Expenses Budget Template

⬇ **Download additional resources on our website at www.librarydirectorstoolkit.com/resources.**

Gerding, S. K., and P. H. Mackellar. *Winning Grants: A How-To-Do-It Manual for Librarians.* 2nd ed. Chicago: ALA Neal-Schuman, 2017.

Hallam, A. *Managing Budgets and Finances: A How-To-Do-It Manual for Librarians and Information Professionals.* New York: Neal-Schuman, 2005.

Rossman, E. A. III. *40+ New Revenue Sources for Libraries and Nonprofits*. Chicago: ALA Editions, 2016.

Sannwald, W. W. *Financial Management for Libraries*. Chicago: ALA Neal-Schuman, 2018.

Smallwood, C. *The Frugal Librarian: Thriving in Tough Economic Times*. Chicago: ALA Editions, 2011.

Smith, G. S. *Managerial Accounting for Libraries and Other Not-for-Profit Organizations*. 2nd ed. Chicago: ALA Editions, 2002.

NOTES

1. Institute of Museum and Library Services (IMLS), "Table 21. Total Operating Revenue of Public Libraries and Percentage Distribution of Revenue, by Source of Revenue and State: Fiscal Year 2012," in *Public Libraries Survey, Fiscal Year 2012*, 58–59, www.imls.gov/assets/1/AssetManager/ FY2012%20PLS_Tables_21_thru_31A.pdf.

2. IMLS, "Table 24. Total Operating Expenditures of Public Libraries and Percentage Distribution of Expenditures, by Type of Expenditure and State: Fiscal Year 2012," in *Public Libraries Survey, Fiscal Year 2012*, 67–68. www.imls.gov/assets/1/AssetManager/FY2012%20PLS_Tables_21_thru_31A.pdf.

3. American Library Association, "Library Operating Expenditures: A Selected Annotated Bibliography," ALA Library Fact Sheet 4, www.ala.org/tools/libfactsheets/alalibraryfactsheet04.

5

LEGAL MATTERS

After reading this chapter, you will know the following:

- How to hire and pay for an attorney
- When to contact an attorney
- The importance of your legal filing dates
- The basics of the Freedom of Information Act and the Open Meetings Act
- How to review and negotiate contracts

All library directors hope they will never need an attorney, but they should always have one they can call upon when the need arises. As with any industry, library attorney specialties vary, and it is important to call an attorney who is an expert in the field related to the topic of concern. It may seem easier to handle the issue yourself in an effort to save money on attorney fees, but this avenue could result in a lawsuit against the library that will cost the library more money in legal fees than if an attorney had been consulted in the first place. You have to know when it is the right time to use an attorney and when it is okay to go it alone.

Every attorney is not created equal. Attorneys specialize in a variety of different areas, and it is imperative that an attorney or law firm be knowledgeable in the area of state library statutes. Other attorney specialties include labor and employment, contract or real estate law, litigation (tort, land use, civil rights, etc.), and municipal law. Once the library engages a law firm, that firm will assign an attorney to the library. When an issue arises that is out of the realm of the contact attorney's expertise, the contact attorney will pull in another attorney from the firm who specializes in the relevant area. In the event that your library does not work with a law firm that covers many specialty areas, create a contact list of attorneys who specialize in the areas that most libraries need: municipal, labor/employment, and contract law.

USING AN ATTORNEY

How do you know when you need to work with an attorney? Not everything needs to have an attorney's hand, but there are times when an attorney should be engaged. An attorney should be used for the following:

- Reviewing policies
- Advising on HR issues (extensive discipline, personal improvement plans, termination)
- Reviewing or advising on complicated Freedom of Information Act requests
- Answering Open Meetings Act questions
- Reviewing ordinances and resolutions, including reviewing levies and budget appropriations
- Creating and reviewing contracts and intergovernmental agreements
- Answering questions on federal laws like the Americans with Disabilities Act, Fair Labor Standards Act, and so on
- Overseeing workers' compensation claims (if insurance company does not provide attorney)
- Consulting or handling (pending) litigation, subpoenas, warrants, or lawsuits
- Developing and reviewing requests for proposals (RFPs)
- Reviewing documentation for referendum and bond issues
- Assisting in the purchase of real estate or annexations

As a library director gains experience and confidence, an attorney is contacted less and less. This is not to say that seasoned library directors don't contact their attorneys. They do; they just know when an issue is something that needs an attorney's opinion.

FINDING AN ATTORNEY

If there is no attorney for the library, or the board is interested in making a change, how do you go about finding an attorney? Choosing the right attorney is important because that person is the professional who will guide you during legal issues and represent you in the event of a lawsuit. A library should have an attorney who specializes in library or municipal law and one who specializes in HR. They may be from the same firm. Most states have statutes specific to public libraries, and having an attorney who is well versed in local library law will save the library money. Find an attorney who is a good fit for your library, board, and community. As the main contact for the library, the director must be comfortable talking and working with the attorney.

Attorneys interpret the law differently. If your library board prefers shorter policies that leave things a little bit more open to interpretation, having an attorney who prefers policies that lay everything out in great detail and use more formal language will not be a good fit. You need to understand the culture of your library and board and find an attorney who matches that culture.

There are many avenues to finding an attorney. Ask other library directors or your library system for recommendations. Contact your city/village government or local school districts and ask whom they use. Regardless of how you gather attorney names, contact them for quotes on their services and to verify their credentials. Most attorneys will create a packet with the law firm's or an individual lawyer's history, practice areas, fees, and, hopefully, a list of current clients. Interview the attorneys and ask questions such as these:

- What is your general response time when you get an inquiry from a client?
- What is your experience in dealing with HR/contracts/building projects (or whatever are your areas of concern, current and future)?
- Do you do your own research or is it passed on to associates or paralegals? (This will affect costs, as associates and paralegals bill at a lesser rate per hour.)
- Do you offer any type of newsletter, podcast, or other form of regular communication?
- How do you handle communications with clients (e.g., e-mail, phone, in person, etc.)?
- How do you keep libraries informed about legislation that affects them?
- How would you handle . . . ? (Pick one or two examples of something that has happened at your library and ask for the attorney's advice.)

Call the references provided by the attorneys and ask the following questions:

- Has the attorney been timely and thorough in responding to your inquiry?
- Are you happy overall with the attorney's services?
- Has the attorney handled HR/contracts/buildings projects or whatever your specific needs are in a satisfactory manner?
- What tone does the attorney use when talking to you?
- Is the attorney's billing concise and accurate?

Once you have vetted the attorneys, it is time to take the matter to the library board. The board should have all the information to make a decision: fees, practice areas, list of clients, answers to the questions asked of the attorneys, and their references. Once you have talked with the attorneys, determine who the best fit is and present that firm or attorney to the board.

Depending on your board, you may not be able to just present your choice. The board may want to interview the candidates. Hiring an attorney is different from hiring a staff member; the board should have a say in who represents the library in legal matters. Once the board has approved the new attorney, contact that attorney to confirm the relationship. If the library had been using a different attorney, contact the previous attorney to let the old attorney know that the library is changing counsel and to send a final invoice, if necessary.

PAYING AN ATTORNEY

Popular culture references suggest that attorneys require a retainer, or a lump sum, before they will perform any work for a client. The attorney then performs work and charges against that retainer until it zeroes out, at which point the work may be completed or the attorney may ask for additional fees to complete the work. Retainers are often used when numerous court appearances or a lot of background work may be necessary.

In the case of a library, the goal is usually to utilize an attorney only when necessary. Most municipal law firms, or attorneys, will charge the library an hourly fee, billed by the quarter hour, when the work is performed. For example, a library director has a sensitive HR issue and is not sure how to handle it legally. The director calls the library attorney for advice, a call that takes twenty-five minutes. The attorney charges $200 per hour and bills by the quarter hour, or any part thereof. The fee for such a consultation will be $100. This may be billed monthly or quarterly, depending on the setup of the attorney's accounting system.

When working on the library budget, it is wise to allocate money for legal fees in the appropriate budget line. If your library is having ongoing legal issues, ask the attorney for an approximate cost on what may be spent in the coming year. If your library rarely uses an attorney, it may be best to set aside funds for five to ten hours of legal services in the event an issue does arise.

CONTACTING THE ATTORNEY

The library director should be the only contact for the library attorney. If board or staff members contact the attorney at will, this can cause confusion for the library and the attorney.

Because time is literally money when talking to the attorney, the discussion needs to be clear and concise. Have the issue and any questions outlined on paper so you can jot down answers as the attorney gives them. It may be helpful to e-mail the question/issue to the attorney in advance so that the attorney can review it and formulate an answer before talking to you. It is a good practice to have a written record of the attorney's advice to present to the board. Even if you call the attorney, you can follow up with an e-mail stating what you understood the attorney's response to be and asking the attorney to respond affirming that this is so.

Having a library attorney is fundamental to making sure the library is covered when there is a legal need, but this does not mean that as a library director you can go about your workday and not worry about legal matters. A library must comply with federal and state employment laws, any and all laws that deal with government entities, and all required resolutions/ordinances and other legal filings. A good library director is aware of and compliant with the local, state, and federal laws that apply to libraries and how they exist as businesses.

EXCEPTION TO THE PRIMARY CONTACT RULE

Although the library director is the main contact for the library attorney, the board president may find it necessary to contact the library attorney directly, typically when there is a personnel matter concerning the library director or when there is no library director on staff. The attorney is the counsel for the library, not the library director, and so is available to handle all library issues as they arise, even if the issue involves the library director.

COMPLYING WITH FEDERAL, STATE, AND LOCAL LAWS

The library, as a business and publicly funded entity, is required to comply with a multitude of federal, state, and local laws. Part of this is making sure that all legal documents are completed and filed correctly and on time. This is a very important aspect of the library director's job. Necessary documents and filing dates will vary from state to state. Many library attorneys will send their clients a listing of required legal filings and dates. If your attorney does not provide this, or you don't have an attorney, contact your library system or state library for the information. If all else fails, look through the previous years' board packets of the library. This should give you an idea of what has been filed in the past.

COMMON FEDERAL AND STATE LAWS

- *Bid requirements for work:* States will have bidding requirements for public entities who hire outside contractors to perform work. Often, if the work to be performed is over a certain dollar amount, the work must be contracted through a public bid process that includes a bid period, publication of the bid request, and an opening of the closed bids during a public meeting. Even if the work is likely to cost less than the legal bid amount, it is still a good practice to obtain a few bids on any work. This keeps contractors' bids competitive and lets the public know the library is being as transparent as possible when hiring out work.

- *Consolidated Omnibus Budget Reconciliation Act (COBRA):* Enacted in 1985, this law allows for employees to continue health care coverage with their employers after separation for a specific amount of time.
- *Department of Labor (DOL):* There is a federal DOL and each state has its own DOL. The U.S. Department of Labor is home to all the federal laws with which employers must comply. Its website is a treasure trove of information for employers and employees alike. Each state's DOL is responsible for state-specific information on laws with which all employers must comply.

DOL POSTER INFORMATION

The U.S. Department of Labor requires that all employers display a current poster of specific information (on FLSA, OSHA, etc.) in a physical place accessible to all staff. Most employers post the information in the lunchroom, near the time clock, or in the staff mailbox area. Posters can be ordered from the DOL and from other agencies or downloaded from their websites. The list of required postings can be found on the DOL website. Check with your state's department of labor for any local posting requirements.

- *Disposal of property:* Each state will have specific parameters on how a public entity is able to dispose of property that has been purchased with taxpayer money. As equipment or furniture gets old and is replaced, there has to be a record of its disposal.
- *Employment Retirement Income Security Act (ERISA):* This law describes regulations for employers who provide retirement benefits for their employees.
- *Equal Employment Opportunity Commission (EEOC):* This separate federal agency works to ensure that employers respect their employees' civil rights. Employees who feel that they have been discriminated against may contact the EEOC for help.
- *Fair Labor Standards Act (FLSA):* This law outlines standards for wage and overtime pay for most employers.
- *Freedom of Information Act (FOIA):* This law provides access to federal government documents by the general public. Each state also has its

own FOIA guidelines, which enable the public to access documents of state and local government organizations.

- *Health Insurance Portability and Accountability Act (HIPAA):* This law provides guidelines on enrolling individuals with pre-existing conditions in health care plans, allows enrollment into a health plan when certain life or work events happen, and prohibits discrimination against employees based on their health status.

- *Open Meetings Act (OMA) and sunshine laws:* The OMA and sunshine laws have been established to provide for transparency in the dealings of government and businesses. The general public is able to observe, and at times may participate in, the meetings and deliberations of government bodies. All states have their own guidelines for sunshine laws.

- *Procurement/purchasing:* As with the disposal of property, there are also standards for purchasing and procuring items.

- *Records retention:* Taxpayer-funded entities are required to retain certain organizational records for a specific amount of time. As with property disposal, there are laws that outline the process for the disposal of library documents. Check with your state library, library system, or attorney for guidelines.

- *Unemployment insurance:* All employers pay into an unemployment pool for their state in the event that a staff member loses his or her job. The rate the employer pays will vary depending on the employer's unemployment record, number of staff, and state guidelines.

- *Workers' compensation:* All employers also pay into a workers' compensation fund to help pay for any staff member who is injured during work. The amount the employer pays is based on the number of employees and their classification (clerk, driver, maintenance, etc.) in addition to the employer's past workers' compensation claims.

HOW TO KEEP UP-TO-DATE ON NEW LAWS

It is important for the library director to keep up-to-date with new laws and HR issues and trends. There are a variety of ways to do this. If your attorney has a blog or newsletter, subscribe to it in order to become aware of new information and laws as they happen. See if your state library or library system has an e-newsletter that you can subscribe to. Being part of a state or national library association is a great way to stay connected and learn about changes to the law.

There are a number of free online newsletters available, and many that you can subscribe to for a fee. The cost to subscribe may be worth it. If your budget is smaller, see if a few libraries will pitch in for one subscription and share the newsletter.

CONTRACTS

The one major legal area that library directors deal with on a regular basis is contracts. The library has a multitude of contracts, from library cards to maintenance agreements. Being vigilant with the library's contracts can save the library a lot of money and future headaches.

The following examples of documents are not standard contracts but should still be treated as such:

- New library card form
- Meeting room request
- Purchase order for furniture or equipment
- Release form to use a piece of equipment, space, a certain type of material, and so on
- Database vendor agreement
- Intergovernmental agreement between two agencies

Each of these is an agreement entered into between two parties and comprises three parts:

Offer: Someone offers to do or not do something.
Consideration: The value being offered makes entering into the contract desirable.
Acceptance: There is an acknowledgment between the two parties that
   they both accept the contract terms.

A contract is made up of terms. The terms explain the promises each party is making and the consequences if the promises are not satisfied. Terms should be clear, straightforward, and unambiguous. Some contracts come from an outside vendor doing business with a library, while some contracts are created within a library.

Most contracts are form documents that are slanted to benefit the vendor and not the library. It is the library director's job to ensure that the needs of the library are being met in the most cost-effective and fair way possible. This may require making changes to that form document. Know that a contract's terms are not written in stone and sealed with blood. The initial contract represents an opening offer that can be negotiated, and most times should be. Never take a contract as final. Ask the vendor for changes to ensure a contract that will be fair to and beneficial for the library.

TERMS TO AVOID

Automatic fee increases: Many vendors have this as a standard part of
   their contracts. For example, "We retain the right to increase the price
   up to XX% or $XXX." This means the library is held to the terms of
   the contract and must continue to pay as the price increases. Try to

CONTRACT DOS AND DON'TS

What to Do with Contracts

While I was working at the New Lenox Public Library District, we started offering a music downloading service to our patrons. After a year, we determined that it was not a service our patrons were excited about and decided to cancel the contract.

When I called to cancel, the company informed us that we could not cancel and had to continue for another year. In reading through the contract, I saw that the termination clause stipulated that we could cancel at any time if we gave thirty days' notice, which we offered to do.

The company was not happy and argued that it was understood that people would give longer notice. I explained that based on the written contract, we did not have to do that. The vendor grudgingly canceled the contract. **—KH**

What Not to Do with Contracts

Early on in my directorship, I signed a contract with a vending company to put in two machines, without reading the contract carefully. After two years or so, we noticed that the customer service had declined immensely and we decided to cancel the service. When I called to cancel, I was informed that since I had not canceled within thirty days of the expiration date of the first year, the contract automatically renewed for an additional six years. We were stuck with the company and could not get out of the contract until reaching the new expiration date of the contract. **—KP**

negotiate for no price increases for the first few years or a cap to the amount that prices can increase annually. This will help in budget preparation for the following years.

Automatic renewal of the contract: This clause requires that if the contract is not canceled within, for example, thirty, sixty, or ninety days prior to the expiration of the contract, it will automatically renew. It could renew for an additional year or even six years. We have seen the cancellation notice set at 180 days prior to the end of the contract. This clause can make it difficult to do a price comparison, as many quotes are applicable for only thirty to sixty days. This clause has become increasingly popular in vendor contracts, likely in the hopes that directors won't read all the fine print.

Indemnification/hold harmless clauses: An indemnification clause obligates a party (or both parties) to compensate the other party for losses or damages set out in the provision. This compensation is separate and apart from other contractual obligations and damages. A hold harmless clause means the two parties cannot sue each other for any damage they may suffer due to the negligence of the other party.

Limitation of liability: The limitation of liability clause restricts the amount and type of damages that one party can recover from another. In vendor-initiated contracts, the limitation of liability will always favor the vendor.

TERMS TO INCLUDE

Scope of work: A detailed description of the work, services, or materials should be included.

Price: As stated in the previous list, you want to be sure to avoid fee increases, but you also want to ensure that the price and any add-ons are included.

Duration of contract: This is the length of the contract. What is a realistic length for any given contract? A seventy-two-month lease for a copier might not be realistic if new technology makes the copier obsolete in forty-eight months. The longer the contract, the longer you will have to wait before changing vendors. However, oftentimes, longer contract terms mean some cost savings.

Insurance/indemnification: This is when one party guarantees payment to another party in the event of a loss or potential loss.

Warranty: This is a written statement that the statements made in a contract are true.

It is in the library's best interest to carefully review contracts, delete anything that will not be advantageous to the library, and add anything that the library needs to have. Many vendors may balk at the idea. Stand firm and remember that the vendor wants the library as a client and will likely negotiate. If a vendor is not willing to compromise, this may be a sign that the vendor will be difficult to work with. Keep in mind that it may be necessary to have the library attorney review the contracts if substantial changes have been made by either party.

The library will have many contracts through the years. Remembering all the terms, costs, and general conditions is difficult, and because it is helpful to have all that data on hand at a moment's notice, create a contract database (download one from our website at www.librarydirectorstoolkit.com/resources) that includes the following:

- Vendor name and address
- Vendor contact name and contact information

- Contract start date
- Termination date
- Notice required for renewal or termination
- Automatic percentage increase (if applicable)
- Date for review (allowing for time to put out for bid, if necessary)
- Addresses for notices
- Cost
- Notes

The library director deals with many legal issues during the course of the job: hiring, termination and staffing issues, and many documents, including contracts and legal filings. Having a working knowledge of federal, state, and local laws that apply to the library in addition to knowing what is necessary to complete all legal filings are a huge part of the work of the library director. Knowing you are not alone helps, too. Having access to an attorney to help navigate complex legal issues will likely save money for the library in the future.

✿ REVIEW AND REFLECT

KEY TAKEAWAYS

Attorneys are necessary, even though we strive to use them only when needed. Use an attorney for the following:

- Reviewing policies
- Advising on HR issues
- Creating and reviewing contracts and intergovernmental agreements
- Answering questions on federal laws
- Consulting or handling (pending) litigation, subpoenas, warrants, or lawsuits

When seeking an attorney, ensure that you find someone with whom you can easily work and who provides clear, concise answers to your questions. Depending on your board, board members may be very involved in the process of hiring an attorney or leave it up to you to decide.

In addition to ensuring that the library has legal representation, a library director must also stay up-to-date on changes in laws. Sign up for local and national newsletters and alerts instead of relying on your attorney to tell you about such changes.

Directors deal with contracts on a regular basis. Being vigilant with the library's contracts can save the library a lot of money and future headaches.

SELF-CHECK

- Do we have a library attorney, and if so, who is it?
- What is the attorney's area of expertise?
- How do I contact our attorney?
- Do we have any pending or open lawsuits?
- Where are all our contracts and what are they for?

QUESTIONS FOR REFLECTION

- Where can I learn more about the laws in my state that affect the library?
- How can I build a contract database?
- What characteristics am I looking for in an attorney?

ADDITIONAL RESOURCES

⤓ **Download a SAMPLE CONTRACT DATABASE and other resources on our website at www.librarydirectorstoolkit.com/resources.**

ADA.gov. "Information and Technical Assistance on the Americans with Disabilities Act." www.ada.gov.

Crews, K., *Copyright Law for Librarians and Educators: Creative Strategies and Practical Solutions*. 4th ed. Chicago: ALA Editions, forthcoming.

HealthCare.gov. The website created as part of the Affordable Care Act, maintained by the U.S. Centers for Medicare & Medicaid Services. www.healthcare.gov.

HR Specialist. www.thehrspecialist.com.

Occupational Safety and Health Administration. A division of the U.S. Department of Labor. www.osha.gov.

Society for Human Resource Management. "SHRM—The Voice of All Things Work." www.shrm.org.

Tucker, V. M., and M. Lampson. *Finding the Answers to Legal Questions*. 2nd ed. Chicago: ALA Neal-Schuman, 2018.

U.S. Department of Labor. www.dol.gov.

U.S. Equal Employment Opportunity Commission. www.eeoc.gov.

6

POLICIES AND PROCEDURES

After reading this chapter, you will know the following:

- The difference between policies and procedures
- Different types of policy manuals you should have
- Key policies you should have for your library
- How to write an effective policy
- How to write effective procedures

P olicies are the guidelines/rules that are used to govern the library, as approved by the board of trustees. Every library should have a group of policies to which staff and patrons can refer. There are three basic groups of policies: general policies, collection management policies, and personnel policies.

Procedures are the instructions for library staff on how to complete different processes within the library, including how to implement library policies. These are some examples of procedures in a library: making a library card for a patron, paying for a lost or damaged book, or inputting patron information into the library patron database system. Library procedures are not approved by the board and may be written down and formed into procedure manuals for different library departments. Policies and procedures are not the same, but they do work in conjunction with each other.

POLICIES

Where do policies come from? While the library board sets policy for the library, it is the library director's responsibility to bring new and updated policies to the board for approval. Library policies are set for the community at large and should not be written in reaction to the actions of an individual or a small group of people.

A well-written policy should:

- align with the library's vision and mission;
- avoid conflict with the library's plans and goals;
- adhere to federal, state, and local laws;
- blend with the library's other policy statements, without contradictions;
- treat all people with fairness and consistency;
- give clear guidance to the director and staff in implementing the policy;
- protect the rights of employees and treat employees with fairness and equity;
- establish overall direction without including procedural aspects;
- reflect best public library practices;
- encourage informed and active decision making by anticipating problems; and
- not be written for exceptions.[1]

The general policies should be reviewed annually, collection management policies every three to five years, and personnel policies every three years. The policy review process need not be long and arduous if you follow these steps:

1. Keep a list of small changes that need to be made as they are noted throughout the year.
2. Review the entire manual for necessary changes.
3. Ask managers to review and provide feedback.
4. Update policies.
5. Have an attorney review the changes.
6. Present revised policies to the board for approval. This does not need to be done all at one time. It may be easier for the board to review and approve a few each month.

TYPES OF POLICIES

There are three main types of policies: general, collection management, and personnel. Another document that is policy adjacent is the strategic plan. More on strategic plans and their role in the library can be found in chapter 11.

General Policies

The general policy manual is public facing and focuses on how the library serves the patrons and community. These policies are what the director and staff will use to set the tone for how the library is used. The following list presents policies you should include in your general policy manual (an asterisk indicates necessary policies):

General policies
- Mission statement*
- Vision statement*
- ALA's Library Bill of Rights*
- ALA Code of Ethics*
- ALA's Core Values of Librarianship*
- ALA's Access to Electronic Information, Services and Networks*
- ALA's Filters and Filtering*
- ALA's Freedom to Read*
- ALA's Freedom to View*
- Administrative/library board
- Board bylaws*
- ALA's Public Library Trustee Ethics Statement
- Freedom of Information Act (FOIA)*
- Friends of the Library
- Identity protection
- Immigration compliance
- Library Records Confidentiality Act*
- Local records retention*
- Travel
- Volunteers

Financial
- Authority to spend*
- Budget and finance
- Gifts/donations*
- Indemnification
- Investment of public funds
- Soliciting and selling

Patrons and library use
- Computers and equipment*
- Copyright restrictions
- Homebound services
- Library materials (circulation, holds/reserves, interlibrary loan, lost or damaged materials)*
- Patron behavior/code of conduct*
- Patron registration*
- Patrons with disabilities*

- Sexual harassment*
- Social media*
- Unattended children/vulnerable persons*

Library facilities
- Closing and holiday schedule*
- Exhibits and displays
- Hours of operation*
- Meeting rooms
- Study rooms

Collection Management Policies

The collection management policies may be included in the general policy manual or may be a separate policy. The collection management policies outline how the library handles the physical and digital collections and how the staff should purchase and discard materials. While primarily intended for internal use, this policy provides information to the community on how the library is spending taxpayer money. These topics are commonly included:

- Purpose of the collection
- Selection of the collection
- Evaluation of the collection
- Censorship
- Request for reconsideration of library material
- Disposal of library materials

Personnel Policies

The personnel policies are intended to help manage the staff. These policies dictate how the library should comply with state and federal laws and outline the conduct expectations and benefits staff will receive. Staff should be required to sign an acknowledgment form indicating that they have received and reviewed the current library personnel policies, and this acknowledgment should be kept in their personnel files. Recommended policies include the following:

Guidelines
- Americans with Disabilities Act
- Attendance and compensation
- Compensatory time (overtime) per the Fair Labor Standards Act
- Disciplinary steps
- Dress code
- Employee evaluations
- Employment-at-will (if an at-will state)

- Equal Employment Opportunity laws
- Health Insurance Portability and Accountability Act
- Meal and rest breaks
- Personnel records (confidentiality of information)
- Reimbursable expenses
- Selection of personnel (authority to hire, reference and background checks, conflict of interest/nepotism)
- Termination of employment
- Timesheet recording
- Workweek

Benefits

- Bereavement leave
- Continuation of health coverage (COBRA)
- Employee assistance program (EAP)
- Family and Medical Leave Act
- Holidays and library closings
- Insurance
  - Dental
  - Health
  - Life
  - Vision
- Jury and witness duty
- Leaves of absence
- Military leave
- Pension
- Short-term and long-term disability
- Sick leave
- Staff library card
- Training and development
- Tuition reimbursement
- Unemployment
- Vacation
- Victims' Economic Security and Safety Act (VESSA)
- Voting time
- Workers' compensation

Conduct

- Antibullying
- Blood-borne pathogens
- Credit card usage
- Drug-free workplace

- Immigration compliance
- Personal vehicle
- Sexual and other forms of harassment
- Smoke-free workplace
- Standards of conduct
- Technology and social media
- Travel
- Whistleblower compliance

Not every library will need every one of these policies. Take a look at your current policy manuals to see what already exists and determine which policies are necessary. Check with your state library or library attorney on what policies are required in your state.

CRAFTING POLICIES

Once it has been determined what policies are needed and which already exist, the rest will have to be created. When writing a policy, start by asking the following questions:

- What is the purpose of this policy?
- What is the scope of this policy?
- Who is the audience for this policy?
- Are there any other similar policies already in existence?
- Is this policy too vague to enforce?
- Is this policy being written with one patron/employee or a very small group of patrons/employees in mind?
- Is this policy consistent with how the library wants to treat patrons/employees?

Policies exist to work as a guide for library staff and patrons and should help to de-escalate situations, not create them. Sometimes what seems like a clear policy will end up being anything but. Utilizing the previous questions will help you craft good policies and avoid some of the common policy pitfalls.

Once these questions are answered, don't immediately start writing the policy; gather sample policies from other libraries to see how they have treated the subject. We recommend that you begin by looking at libraries of similar size, both in your area and out of state, to get a wide range of examples and then create a list of the libraries with policies that would be the best fit. While libraries share freely, the downside to using other libraries' policies is that the wording can become inconsistent with your other policies. For instance, one policy might use "customer" while another might use "patron." Remember to change the wording of borrowed policies to be consistent with the terminology used in your existing policies.

After reviewing policies from other libraries and marking sections that will work in the policy you are drafting, start writing your policy. To help maintain consistency, create a policy template that can be used for each new policy:

- Type of policy (general, collection, personnel)
- Policy section (e.g., guidelines, benefits, conduct)
- Policy name (may also include a number for easy reference)
- Policy creation date (when the board approved the policy)
- Policy update dates
- Purpose of policy (if needed)
- Policy content

Begin each policy on a new page. Having each one separate will make it easier to update all manuals when it is time to update individual policies.

To create the most effective policies, keep these tips in mind:

Keep it simple. Keep the purpose of the policy at the forefront. Don't add in every possibility to the policy. Remember, this is a guiding document, not a comprehensive training manual for every situation that could arise.

Be concise. Don't create a three-page policy when a three-paragraph policy will work. Remember that people will be referencing these policies to help them know what to do in different situations. Make sure they are easy to scan to glean the main points.

Avoid abbreviations and acronyms. Not everyone is familiar with library or legal terms. Remember to write out everything in full so people reading the policies know what you are talking about.

Be consistent. Keep a style manual for common words used (e.g., patron versus customer) and pay attention to grammar, punctuation, and format (e.g., font face and size).

Revise when necessary. Policies are not written in stone. Go back and revise any policies that don't work the way they were intended. Policies are living documents that change as the library's needs change.

Refer to part II, "Tools," for some sample policies.

APPROVING POLICIES

Once the policies are completed, have them reviewed by the library attorney. While having the attorney review the policy might seem like an unnecessary expense, this step can save major headaches down the road and help to avoid having any policies that do not comply with local, state, or federal law. There will also be times when a law changes and a policy may need to be revised before the annual review. If the library has an attorney who specializes in libraries and/or municipal law, the attorney will likely keep you up-to-date on any changes to laws that require new policies and will also often provide a sample policy. You can also check with your regional library system or state library to see if either has a sample that you can use.

Once the attorney has reviewed a policy, bring it to the board for approval. Depending on the library board's structure, a policy committee might review policies prior to review by the entire board. Some boards pay very close attention to policies and ask for many revisions, while others choose just to approve them as is. During the board meeting, if a board member wants a change, you don't have to wait until next month to get approval on the revision. When making the motion, the board member can state, "Motion to approve the policy as amended" and then include what is being changed so that there is a record of the change in the board meeting minutes. If the policy change is going to have a significant impact on patrons, have the board member making the motion state in the motion when the policy is going into effect: "Motion to approve the updated circulation policy and eliminate overdue fines as of May 1, 2019."

After the board has approved the new or updated policy, it should be shared with staff and patrons; make sure to post all policies on the website in order to be transparent with patrons about your expectations for them. Some policies have more impact than others. In the case of circulation policy changes (e.g., eliminating overdue fines), create a plan to communicate the change and when it is taking place. Make sure staff are aware of policy changes, and share where copies of the new policies are going to be located. For policies that don't have as much of an impact on staff or patrons, still let the staff know that changes have taken place, but don't spend as much time explaining the new policies. However, no matter what the change, always inform staff why a policy is being adopted and the purpose of that policy.

PROCEDURES

While policies are the guiding principles of the library, procedures are how those policies play out in the day-to-day operations of the library. Procedures may also be outlined in training manuals. Procedures not only are helpful for new and existing staff but also provide needed documentation for succession planning. Procedures can take many forms, but a template for library-wide procedures that includes the following can help ensure consistency:

- Procedure name
- Date created/updated
- File path—where the procedure is stored if online

- Purpose—one to two sentences on the goal of the procedure
- General information—general overview and basic information staff need to consider before following the steps of the policy
- Procedure—the list of steps for staff to complete, listed chronologically, by department, or by workflow, depending on the complexity of the procedure

When training new staff or handling personnel issues, procedures help provide a framework for expectations. Procedure manuals should be stored in a central location for library-wide procedures and in specific locations for departmental procedures. Having a staff intranet or network drive allows all staff access to the procedures they need to do their jobs effectively. This type of resource can include the following procedural information:

- Americans with Disabilities Act (ADA)
- Cataloging (including processing)
- Circulation (new library cards, holds processing, nonresident cards)
- Customer service standards
- Emergency manual
- ILS training manuals
- Meeting and study room bookings
- Opening and closing schedules for the library
- Programming (current programs, registration, cancellation, etc.)
- Purchasing (materials, supplies, equipment, etc.)
- Social media (for library accounts)
- Style and branding guide
- Telephone directory
- Timesheet records
- Vacation and sick time requests

There may be no written procedures for routine library tasks or there may be a manual that is very old. Each department should have documented procedures for routine tasks in addition to the library-wide procedures. Documenting procedures and creating a manual can be accomplished as a collaborative effort between the director and staff.

✿ REVIEW AND REFLECT

KEY TAKEAWAYS

Policies are set by the board and govern the library. Procedures tell staff how to enact policies and perform specific tasks.

You will have three policy manuals:

- General policies are for patrons and govern the running of the library.
- Collection management policies provide staff with guidelines on how to purchase, maintain, and weed collections.
- Personnel policies guide staff on employee responsibilities and benefits.

When crafting policies, consider the purpose, scope, and audience before researching sample policies. Ensure each policy is consistent with how the library wants to treat patrons/employees.

SELF-CHECK

- Where are our general policy, collection development policy, and personnel policy manuals located?
- When were our policy manuals last updated?
- Are our policies posted on our website?
- What procedures do we have in place?
- How do staff access policies and procedures for reference?

QUESTIONS FOR REFLECTION

- Does our library have a comprehensive general policy manual? Collection development policy manual? Personnel policy manual?
- What policies are missing or need to be updated?
- Do I, my staff, and the board of trustees evaluate library policies on a regular basis?
- What procedures do I need to write?

ADDITIONAL RESOURCES

See part II for these additional resources on policies and procedures:

- Sample 6.1: Public Code of Behavior Policy
- Sample 6.2: Unattended Children and Vulnerable Adults Policy
- Sample 6.3: Gifts and Donations Policy

⬇ **Download additional resources on our website at www.librarydirectorstoolkit.com/resources.**

American Library Association. "Access to Electronic Information, Services, and Networks: An Interpretation of the Library Bill of Rights." www.ala.org/advocacy/sites/ala.org.advocacy/files/content/intfreedom/librarybill/interpretations/accesstoelectronic.pdf.

———. "Code of Ethics of the American Library Association." www.ala.org/united/sites/ala.org
.united/files/content/trustees/orgtools/policies/ALA-code-of-ethics.pdf.

———. "Core Values of Librarianship." www.ala.org/advocacy/intfreedom/corevalues.

———. "Filters and Filtering." www.ala.org/advocacy/intfreedom/filtering.

———. "The Freedom to Read Statement." www.ala.org/advocacy/intfreedom/
freedomreadstatement.

———. "Freedom to View Statement." www.ala.org/rt/vrt/professionalresources/vrtresources/
freedomtoview.

———. "Library Bill of Rights." www.ala.org/advocacy/intfreedom/librarybill.

Brumley, R. *The Public Library Manager's Forms, Policies, and Procedures Manual with CD-ROM*.
New York: Neal-Schuman, 2004.

Larson, J. C., and H. L. Totten. *The Public Library Policy Writer: A Guidebook with Model Policies
on CD-ROM*. New York: Neal-Schuman, 2008.

Nelson, S., and J. M. Garcia. *Creating Policies for Results: From Chaos to Clarity*. Chicago: ALA
Editions, 2003.

NOTE

1. Adapted from Washington State Library, *Public Library Trustee Reference Manual* (Olympia, WA:
Washington State Library, 2001), www.sos.wa.gov/library/libraries/libdev/publications.aspx#man.

7

INSURANCE

After reading this chapter, you will know the following:

- The different types of insurance and what they are for
- Health and liability insurance terms
- Common insurance policies to have in place
- How to determine the appropriate coverage
- How to buy insurance from different sources

I nsurance—just its mention can cause glazed eyes in many conversations. As in your personal life, your library needs different types of insurance coverage. If you have a facility, you need public liability coverage. If you have employees, health insurance is a preferred benefit. Having staff means getting coverage for unemployment and workers' compensation. If the library owns a vehicle, such as a van or bookmobile, it, too, must be covered by insurance. You and your board need insurance coverage in the event a mistake is made while making administrative decisions. The library may also choose to have coverage in the event an employee steals money from the library. Now libraries are finding they need cyber liability in the event library servers are hacked and patron and/or financial information is stolen.

Since insurance is something that all libraries need, as the library director, you need to know what types are available and what they cover before you can determine the appropriate coverage for your library. Then you will need to know how to purchase insurance and what to do to ensure you are getting a good price for your coverage. While we aim to avoid assumptions, with insurance, one assumption can be made: your insurance premiums will trend in one direction—up.

First, we look at the different types of insurance, with a focus on two primary areas of insurance: health and liability. While most people are familiar with health insurance, liability insurance can be more nuanced. After learning about different types, we will look at what coverage you should have and then go over how to buy insurance from different sources.

HEALTH INSURANCE

Health insurance—the holy grail of full-time employees. Most employees desire full-time positions so that they can qualify for health insurance benefits. The 2010 Patient Protection and Affordable Care Act, more commonly known as just the Affordable Care Act or ACA, requires employers to provide health care coverage if they have more than fifty full-time equivalent (FTE) employees. Check with your attorney or insurance provider to determine whether you need to comply with ACA regulations.

HEALTH INSURANCE TERMS TO KNOW

Copay: A copay is a set amount a patient pays each time the patient visits the doctor ($20, $40, etc.) for services. Copays are standard in HMOs (health maintenance organizations). Once a patient pays a copay, the patient usually is not responsible for paying any other charges related to that visit. In addition to copays, other charges during the year include monthly premiums and fees for services obtained outside the HMO's provider network. In a PPO (preferred provider organization), a patient's copay may be applied to the annual deductible.

Deductible: The deductible is the amount a patient must pay before the health insurance company picks up the remainder of the cost for care. Deductibles can vary greatly in price depending on the type of insurance.

In network: This term applies to medical professionals and facilities that have contracted with a health insurance company. The insurance company typically negotiates specific rates for their members with medical professionals and/or facilities in a particular region. A patient can expect to pay a set amount or percentage rate for a visit to any provider in the network.

Out of network: This term applies to medical professionals and facilities that have not contracted with a health insurance company to provide services at negotiated rates. A provider that is not in the insurance company's assigned network is considered out of network. A patient can expect to pay a higher amount or percentage rate for a visit to any provider who is out of network.

Premium: A premium is the amount that a person pays for health insurance each month. Oftentimes, the employer will pay a portion of the premium to help offset the cost to the employee.

Health insurance is a significant cost for most employers, and administrators need to keep those costs as manageable as possible. A library may not have as many full-time employees in an effort to mitigate its health insurance responsibility. Many employers require their employees to pay a portion of the monthly premium for either themselves or covered family members, while some may be able to cover costs only for the employee. The cost breakdown and choices your library can offer are largely based on the kinds of plans you have, their costs, the number of employees who need coverage, and your overall budget. A sample breakdown of health insurance costs appears in table 7.1.

Employers with a large staff benefit from the greater buying power they have based on the number of staff they insure. Smaller libraries do not have such large numbers of full-time employees and can be at a disadvantage for getting more competitive quotes. When they do not have a large pool of employees to insure, libraries can consider joining a library health insurance cooperative pool if one is available to them, which helps lower costs by increasing the number of people covered.

Employers must also check on local, state, and federal laws concerning health care coverage. You may have different requirements based on your location and need to ensure you are complying with the law. Health care coverage can be tricky, so we recommend checking with your local attorney on your requirements.

Once you have determined who is covered, you have to choose what type of plan(s) to offer staff. Here are some of the plan types you might consider for coverage:

- Health maintenance organization (HMO)
- Preferred provider organization (PPO)
- Health savings account (HSA)
- Flexible spending account (FSA)

TABLE 7.1 Sample Costs for Health Insurance

HMO COVERAGE	TOTAL MONTHLY COST (Annual Cost)	EMPLOYEE MONTHLY COST (Annual Cost)	LIBRARY MONTHLY COST (Annual Cost)
Employee (80% covered by library)	$621 ($7,452)	$124 ($1,490)	$497 ($5,962)
Employee and Spouse (50% covered by library)	$1,334 ($16,008)	$667 ($8,004)	$667 ($8,004)
Employee and Child(ren) (50% covered by library)	$1,254 ($15,048)	$627 ($7,524)	$627 ($7,524)
Family (35% covered by library)	$1,940 ($23,280)	$1,261 ($15,132)	$679 ($8,148)

HEALTH MAINTENANCE ORGANIZATION

An HMO allows access to doctors and services within a certain network for lower-cost premiums. The professionals in the network consent to an agreed upon cost for services for patients who see them. The goal is to give an acceptable standard of care at reasonable cost to the insured. Any specialized doctors or work must be referred and/or approved by a patient's primary care physician for the plan to pay for the charges. If the insured goes out of network without prior approval, the charges will likely not be covered, with the exception of an emergency. If the charges are covered, it may be only a small amount, with the remainder being the responsibility of the patient.

An HMO is a great option for someone who is fairly healthy and visits the doctor infrequently. HMOs are often the health plan of choice for younger individuals or for people with less disposable income. Before deciding whether to offer an HMO to staff, consider your demographics and whether your staff will be interested in this type of plan.

Benefits

- The premiums are normally less expensive, and there is usually no deductible at the time of the office visit, or you may be billed later for services rendered.
- There is usually a copay for prescription drugs at the time of purchase, but it is generally a nominal cost.

Drawbacks

- If a patient has specific needs that require more specialized care or a greater number of visits, or if a patient wants to go to any doctor the patient chooses, having an HMO is likely not the best option.
- HMOs often have more restrictions on the number of visits, tests, and/or specialized treatments.

PREFERRED PROVIDER ORGANIZATION

A PPO allows more flexibility in the providers and/or services to which a patient has access. There is still a primary network, but PPOs offer more flexibility if you want to go out of network for a certain doctor or treatment. Patients don't need to get prior approval from a primary care physician for services or treatments. This flexibility usually comes at a cost. The premiums for a PPO plan are often higher than they are for an HMO. There may also be a deductible, depending on the plan. Patients may have a copay at the time of an office visit or be billed at a later date. Normally any copay is applied to the annual deductible. Once that deductible is met, the patient may have no further costs for standard services or tests, or depending on the plan, these may be covered by a percentage split (80/20, 70/30, etc.) between the library and the employee.

Benefits

- A PPO is an excellent plan if a patient wants to have a choice of doctors, has more specialized needs, and/or has more disposable income.

Drawbacks

- PPOs are often much more expensive than HMOs.

HEALTH SAVINGS ACCOUNTS

HSAs are specific to a high-deductible PPO, which is a plan with a deductible that is higher than the average PPO deductible. A regular PPO may have a $1,000/$1,500 deductible, but a high-deductible PPO could be $2,500 or higher. HSAs are available only to people who also have a high-deductible PPO. With an HSA, pretax money is put into an account and can be used only to pay for health care expenses (deductibles, prescriptions, tests, etc.). Employers will often contribute to the staff members' HSAs to help offset the cost of the deductible for the staff members. The employer contribution could be as much as half or more of the deductible. Much will depend on the PPO and the savings the employer gains by employees signing up for a high-deductible PPO. An HSA combined with a high-deductible PPO usually has a much lower premium than a traditional PPO plan, which can make them attractive to employers.

Employees may also contribute to these accounts to increase their account balances. Employees receive tax benefits for contributing annually to their HSAs. The balance in an HSA can be rolled over each year (unlike with an FSA) and go with the employee when changing jobs or leaving the workforce.

There is a learning curve for an HSA. The plan is contingent on the employee shopping for specific medical services. For example, if the employee needs an MRI (magnetic resonance imaging) scan, it might be more cost-effective to go to an independent MRI office than to get one at a hospital. The HSA plan will usually offer a benefits advisor to help patients work through finding the best costs for the services they need. When employees are contributing to their savings and/or spending their own money, they are more likely to be good consumers. There are annual maximum contributions that are allowed by the IRS (Internal Revenue Service). Be sure to check the latest IRS rules on those contributions. Your bank will also know the maximum allowable per year.

Benefits

- Any amount contributed by an employee into the HSA account is pretax money, which means that their taxable income is lower.
- Premiums for an HSA can be less expensive than for other plans, which is a cost savings for employers.
- Because the premiums may be less, an employer may contribute monies to the employees' HSA accounts, which can be used toward the deductible

or other health costs in an effort to encourage employees to sign up for the high-deductible PPO plan. So if employee doesn't go to the doctor often, this is an excellent way to build up the HSA.

■ HSAs are portable and not tied to a specific employer. Employees can leave their jobs and continue to contribute to their HSAs as long as they choose.

Drawbacks

■ HSAs present a big learning curve for employees who have utilized HMOs or traditional PPOs in the past.

■ Deductibles can be quite expensive and cost prohibitive.

■ Employees may spend more time shopping around for less expensive medical tests, and so forth, in an effort to manage their health care costs.

■ Money in an HSA can be used only for medical needs.

FLEXIBLE SPENDING ACCOUNTS

FSAs are similar to HSAs in that the monies deposited are pretax, they can be used for medical expenses, and both the employer and employee can contribute. However, FSAs do not have to be tied to a specific medical plan, and the monies are under an annual "Use it or lose it" provision. Employers will use this as an additional benefit for staff. Since an FSA is not tied to a specific plan, the monies can be used for copays, medications, or elective treatments that may not be covered by insurance (e.g., LASIK surgery).

An FSA requires staff to be consumer conscious. There are also annual maximum contribution allowances for an FSA, so be sure to check with the bank or the IRS website to see what they are.

Benefits

■ Any amount contributed by an employee into the FSA is pretax money, which lowers the employee's taxable income.

■ Premiums for an FSA can be less expensive than for other plans, which is a cost savings for employers.

■ Because the premiums may be less, an employer may contribute monies to employees' FSA accounts, which can be used toward the deductible or other health costs in an effort to encourage employees to sign up. FSAs are not tied to a specific type of insurance (e.g., HMO, PPO) like an HSA is.

Drawbacks

■ The funds in an FSA do not roll over each year; you must use it or lose it by year's end.

All insurance plans have pros and cons. Libraries need to make the decision on what to offer based on what best fits their finances and staff needs. These needs may change over time, and the library should be able to adjust insurance coverage as well. Consider reviewing your plan at least every other year to ensure you are not only getting competitive pricing but also offering your employees a good choice.

LIABILITY INSURANCE

Depending on how many staff the library has, health insurance may be a large portion of the library budget, but there are other insurance coverages a library must have, and these fall under the category of liability insurance. This type of insurance is outward facing and covers the patrons, board and staff members, and the building and its contents. Liability insurance has many pieces, but the largest is public liability insurance.

PUBLIC LIABILITY INSURANCE

Public liability insurance is what covers the building and grounds, the contents of the building, library vehicles, and any accidents involving patrons on library property. It is important to have adequate coverage in the event of a major claim. It is also important that a library not be underinsured or overinsured. Being underinsured will cause the library to have to make up for that lesser coverage in the event of a claim; being overinsured is not beneficial to the library as it costs more in premiums when the coverage may not be necessary. Ask colleagues of similarly sized libraries in your region about their coverages and premiums to get an idea of the amount of coverage you may need.

There are various coverages included in your liability insurance. You've got your building and contents, but you also have coverage for incidents caused by your HVAC system, which is called "boiler and machinery" coverage. If you have any vehicles, such as a bookmobile or van, you will need automobile coverage. Some states may require flood insurance if you are in a floodplain. Coverage can be purchased for just about anything—mold, terrorism, marine disasters—whatever your needs may be.

It is a good idea to have a building appraisal done to determine the worth of your facility and grounds. The appraisal should include all your furnishings, equipment, materials collection, and any art. You can hire an outside appraisal company to perform this service, which should be done every four to six years or whenever you have a major building change. An up-to-date appraisal is also helpful for your auditor when creating and maintaining your depreciation schedule for all your long-term assets.

CYBER LIABILITY COVERAGE

A newer coverage has emerged in the past few years in light of the increasing security breaches of financial and other institutions' networks, ransomware attacks, and other

LIABILITY INSURANCE TERMS TO KNOW

Business personal property: This type of coverage can also be called contents. Contents covers the building and what is in it—equipment, furniture, materials, and so on.

Deductible: The deductible is what must be paid before the insurance company picks up the remainder of the cost. Generally, the lower the deductible, the higher the annual premium.

General aggregate: This is the total amount an insurance company will pay out during a policy term, usually one year. There may be several claims for one year, but the claims cannot exceed the general aggregate limit. If the aggregate limit is reached, the insured usually has to make up the remaining claim amount out of pocket.

Policy limit: This is the total amount an insurance company will pay during a policy term, usually one year. Normally, the policy will state a policy limit or an aggregate limit.

Umbrella policy: An umbrella policy gives you additional coverage beyond what your standard policy covers for an additional fee. Many businesses have an umbrella policy. For example, a library may have $1 million in coverage and an additional $3 million in umbrella coverage.

cyber threats. Institutions, including libraries, have become increasingly more dependent on technology, so there is a need to protect that technology and our ability to use it. Recovering from a breach means far more than putting your network and IT infrastructure right. If anyone's personal information is accessed and/or stolen as part of a breach, federal law requires the breached institution to pay for one year of credit monitoring for every person affected by the breach. You will also need to craft and release media messages addressing the breach. Public relations can be an important component to combatting the panic that can sometimes arise in the wake of a cyber breach.

In addition to these factors, it can be very costly for your IT people to repair the breached infrastructure. Entire servers may have to be rebuilt, and while this is being completed, a library still has to have access to technology. Temporary servers may need to be brought in and configured. Computers may need to be cleaned of viruses and restored. All these additional costs will be paid out by your cyber liability insurance coverage.

DIRECTORS AND OFFICERS INSURANCE

Directors and officers (D&O) insurance is coverage for any claims made against you (as the library director) or the board for any unintentional wrongful acts that may occur during the course of making decisions for the library.

Library directors make decisions based on the most and best information they have at the time. As stewards of public funds, directors should be as careful as possible when making decisions. However, there are times when directors will need to make a decision without all the information available, only to find out later that it was the wrong decision. In such cases, the library director or board of trustees can be sued. This is when D&O coverage comes into play. It covers the parties doing their jobs as library representatives and not as private citizens. This does not mean that someone can't sue the library director or a trustee as a private citizen, but the D&O insurance will help mitigate the issue.

GOVERNMENT CRIME COVERAGE

Government crime insurance will cover your staff and any theft or financial errors they may make as employees who come into contact with money at your library. Government crime coverage can also include your treasurer and board of trustees, therefore eliminating the need for the separate treasurer's bond. This coverage is usually more expensive than the treasurer's bond, but it offers comprehensive coverage for all library employees, which can make it worth the cost.

NOTARY PUBLIC SURETY BOND

A notary public surety bond is coverage underwritten by an insurance company in the event you or any of the library staff are notary publics. Most states require that notaries be bonded by an insurance company because they perform the duties of a notary in good faith. Often this bond can be obtained through your public liability insurer.

TREASURER'S BOND

In most states, the treasurer of your board must be covered by a bond issued by an insurance company. Since the treasurer is the person officially responsible for signing off on all the finances and financial documents of the library, independent coverage is necessary. Depending on your state's laws, that bond could be as much as half of your annual budget. This bond is to cover any errors made by your treasurer beyond the D&O insurance.

UNEMPLOYMENT INSURANCE

If you have staff, you need unemployment insurance. You are required to pay into the state unemployment fund for every staff member you have in the event that a staff member becomes unemployed through no fault of his or her own. The amount you pay is based on how many staff members you have, your past history of laying people off, and the current tax rate.

When a staff member is downsized or terminated for cause, that employee will likely file for unemployment. As the director looking out for the library, you should fight an unemployment claim. If the staff member wins, that claim will go against your employer's unemployment record, which will increase your unemployment rates in coming years.

WORKERS' COMPENSATION

Workers' compensation ensures wage replacement and payment for necessary medical treatment if a staff member is injured at the workplace or while on work time at another location. Staff are paid a percentage of their salary in the event of a workers' compensation claim. As with unemployment, the library's workers' compensation premiums are based on the library's number of staff and their subsequent salaries, workers' compensation claim history, and tax rate. Most workers' compensation insurance companies perform an annual audit to ensure that you have the appropriate coverage. Coverage for maintenance employees is typically higher than that for other employees.

A workers' compensation claim can be made when a staff member is injured while at the workplace or while performing work duties at another location. Should an incident occur with a staff member, you should fill out an accident/incident report and call the insurance company immediately to file a claim. (A sample accident/incident report is included in part II, "Tools.") The insurance company's claims office will direct you as to the next steps. Be aware that the insurance company determines whether an accident counts as a workers' compensation claim or not. The library has no say in that determination, which can be difficult if you feel a claim is justified but your insurance carrier denies it.

BUYING INSURANCE

Insurance is necessary for any library, but how do you purchase it? As with your personal auto or home insurance, some insurance companies specialize in business insurance coverage. There are usually three options for purchasing insurance:

- Local insurance agent
- Insurance broker
- Insurance pool

LOCAL INSURANCE AGENT

Many libraries like to keep business local and as such may use a local agent to supply their insurance needs. Most local agents should have business coverage available in addition to personal coverage. One of the benefits to using a local agent is the relationship that can develop over time. Often you will know your agent personally, and when a claim happens, you will likely get immediate, personalized service. Your agent can help you through the claims process and any hurdles that may follow.

The downside is that a local agent may not have the ability to be as competitive in pricing or coverage options as a larger agent or broker or may not be as informed about coverage for libraries or municipalities. Your decision on whom to hire will depend on the hiring philosophy employed by you and your board. We recommend soliciting quotes every few years to ensure the coverage and pricing are appropriate for your library's needs, even when using a local agent.

INSURANCE BROKER

Insurance brokers are specialists who work on your behalf to get you the most competitive quote available. They navigate the many different insurance vendors and negotiate prices. Brokers are there to help you understand the coverage available and to construct a plan that provides the coverage you need. They work for you, not the insurance companies, and it is in their best interests to help you find the best deals. Using a broker is a way to maximize your monies, since the broker works for you and will find you the lowest rates with the best coverage. By searching all the insurance companies available, a broker ensures that companies are competitive in offering benefits and in providing lower insurance rates. Because your broker is working with multiple insurance companies, the broker can recommend new coverage and help you discover the best deals. Look for a broker who works with governmental agencies as such a broker will have more awareness of the types of coverage you will need.

INSURANCE POOL

An insurance pool is a group of libraries or other municipalities that come together, either through an insurance agent or on their own, in order to spread the risk among more entities. Many libraries may not be large enough to allow for competitive quotes when seeking insurance on their own. A library that joins a pool has more leverage based on having more buying power. Insurance companies may offer pools more favorable quotes because they know they will get more premiums with a larger group. Libraries are also a fairly safe market for insurance companies. Libraries normally don't have many claims in regard to liability, and that makes them a safe bet. Low claims plus more premiums makes money for insurance companies, and this can translate to stable and sometimes lower premiums for libraries.

Pools have the benefits of stability and consistent coverage. Many libraries, schools, park districts, and municipalities form insurance pools to conserve fiscal resources. However, a caveat to joining an insurance pool is that a library may be bound to the pool for an extended period of time (years) and may not get to choose the amount of coverage offered or how much that coverage will increase annually. Many pools also require that all members have the same coverage, which means a library can end up with too much or unnecessary coverage. Each library will have to determine the best way to move forward with insurance pools.

So, how do you choose which type of insurance plan to go with? Each offers different benefits, and you will need to decide which is most appropriate based on your board's preference, your comfort level, and past practices at your library. If you are feeling unsure about what to do, don't forget to call on neighboring libraries and ask lots of questions until you feel comfortable making a solid decision.

✿ REVIEW AND REFLECT

KEY TAKEAWAYS

Libraries require different types of insurance for staff and liability:

- Health insurance, which may include dental and vision
- Life insurance, which some libraries choose to provide
- Public liability for your facility, crime coverage, cyber security, finances, and officers
- Unemployment insurance
- Workers' compensation

These are important health insurance terms to know:

- Health maintenance organization
- Preferred provider organization
- Health savings account
- Flexible spending account

Libraries have to determine how they want to purchase their insurance coverage. It can be purchased through a local insurance agent, through an insurance broker, or by joining an insurance pool.

SELF-CHECK

- Who do we get our health insurance from?
- Who provides our liability insurance?
- Where are the insurance documents located?
- What policies do we have in place?
- Who provides our insurance? Local agent? Broker? Pool?

QUESTIONS FOR REFLECTION

- Do we have adequate coverage in all the different areas?
- Is there any coverage that we should have but don't?
- Are we offering the best combination of insurance for our health care needs?

ADDITIONAL RESOURCES

See part II for this additional resource on insurance:

- Sample 7.1: Incident and Accident Report Form

⬇ **Download additional resources on our website at www.librarydirectorstoolkit.com/resources.**

Keeton, R., A. Widiss, and J. Fischer. *Insurance Law: A Guide to Fundamental Principles, Legal Doctrines and Commercial Practices.* 2nd ed. Saint Paul, MN: West Academic, 2016.

Redja, G., and M. McNamara. *Principles of Risk Management and Insurance.* 13th ed. London: Pearson, 2016.

8

BUILDINGS

After reading this chapter, you will know the following:

- Where to go to learn about all the library's maintenance systems for your building
- How to keep your building clean
- What you need to know about building maintenance for emergencies
- What general maintenance you need to plan for
- What larger capital projects you need to plan for in the future
- How to create a capital improvement plan for your building

Your library facility is the most expensive physical asset your organization has. Thousands or even millions of people will walk through the doors in its lifetime, utilizing the furniture and equipment on a daily basis. All of this traffic causes wear and tear on the facility and its contents.

Maintaining the building, equipment, and furnishings is necessary to make sure the building and its systems last as long as possible. In a perfect world, every library has full-time staff who can keep the building clean and ensure that all the building systems are running smoothly, but this is usually not the case. Larger buildings or well-funded libraries will likely have full-time cleaning and/or maintenance staff, but most libraries will have either part-time staff or no formal maintenance person. Ultimately, you are responsible for ensuring the building is maintained. Ignoring small issues will result in larger issues that will cost the library down the road. Even if you have maintenance staff, you still need a basic understanding of how your building works.

BUILDING MAINTENANCE SYSTEMS

Where do you start? A thorough knowledge of all the library systems is necessary to keep the building maintained. Reviewing a copy of the blueprints, as-built drawings, or, at minimum, floor plans of your facility is a good place to start. Hopefully, you have access to one or all of these documents. If not, check with your city or village to see whether copies of these exist in the government archives. If that doesn't work, then contact the architect who designed the building. The architect should have paper or digital files of all the work related to the library. The blueprints will list the date created; show all mechanical, plumbing, electrical, and fire protection systems in the building; and give you a good starting point to get familiar with the facility.

Most libraries have annual contracts with vendors to evaluate and repair most systems. These annual contracts are preventative in nature, and vendors will inform the maintenance staff and/or library director if any necessary repairs will be needed in the foreseeable future. Such contracts are not inexpensive, but doing preventative maintenance will allow you to plan for repairs rather than have them spring up on you. Knowing about any repairs or replacements in advance is necessary so that the library director and board can plan for future expenditures. This is where a capital improvement plan comes into play, which we discuss in more detail later in this chapter. Take a look at your service contracts. If you can't find them, look at your past few years of invoices and then call the companies that provide service for your maintenance systems and ask them to provide you with copies.

Relying on the service contracts alone is not enough. Becoming familiar with the facility's systems and maintenance schedule is a key part of the knowledge you must

COMMON BUILDING MAINTENANCE SYSTEMS

Most libraries have the following mechanical systems:

- HVAC (heating, ventilation, and air conditioning)
- Electrical (depending on the size of the library, possibly several electrical panels in different parts of the building)
- Plumbing (hot water heaters)
- Fire suppression (either water sprinklers or dry chemicals)

Larger library facilities may have the following:

- Boiler
- Several hot water heaters
- Irrigation system for landscaping
- Elevator

gain as a library director. If you are lucky enough to have a facility manager, plan a tour of the building and discuss the maintenance schedule. While you may not be setting the appointments for maintenance, you will be approving the contracts and respective invoices for those appointments and answering any questions the board may have on them, so being familiar with these aspects is necessary.

If you do not have a maintenance person, get to know your facility vendors. They are often very helpful in explaining systems and can help you troubleshoot issues. They will also give you an idea of how long a situation can go before remediation is necessary. Most of the vendors who work with libraries understand the budget constraints libraries face and are usually willing to work with them.

Some of the most important areas of your building to locate are the shutoff valves for any water, electrical, and gas systems. Your managers and other staff should also know where these are and how to turn them off. There will come a time when a toilet will not stop flushing or will pull away from the wall, and knowing the location of the shut-off valve will help minimize water damage. Some shut-off valves require a special tool. Know where that is and how to use it. If possible, have two of any special tool on hand as one will inevitably be misplaced or lost.

Know the location of your main electrical breaker box. Depending on the size of your facility, there may be multiple electrical boxes, but there is always one main shut-off switch for the entire property. When dealing with natural gas, know that the fumes are highly combustible and getting to that shut-off valve quickly may help prevent an explosion. Not every building has natural gas and may use electric to heat the water or furnace so be sure to check which system is in your building.

Be sure to show your emergency personnel the location of all shut-off valves and electrical boxes. Some municipalities may require signs be posted to indicate where they are located and the status of annual inspections. If you are new to your job, walk around with the inspectors; they can point out the important things to you.

A BUILDING CAUTIONARY TALE

Weeks after we had opened the new library to the public, I got a call from the staff as the library was closing on Saturday night. One of the toilets in the men's washroom would not stop flushing. The maintenance person was on vacation and not answering his phone. I drove out to the library to see what to do. Neither I nor staff could find the water shut-off valve for the toilet. I called a plumber to come; and since it was a Saturday night, it was considered an emergency call and I was told a plumber would get there when he could. I waited about seven hours for the plumber to arrive, as the toilet continued to flush. Between the costs for the emergency call and the water used, the library spent nearly $500. *—KP*

CLEANING YOUR FACILITY

Beyond ensuring that the larger systems are maintained, you must also ensure that your facility is cleaned on a regular basis. This is not only to maintain the looks of the facility but also for health reasons. Surfaces get dirty with so many people using them, and dust gathers from books, shoes, and the doors opening constantly. A clean library will help patrons and staff stay healthier, and it will help keep the building from falling into disrepair.

Maintaining a clean library may be done by library staff, an outside company, or a combination of the two. To help keep your library sparkling, create checklists for the work to be performed by the outsourced cleaning vendor and/or library cleaning staff so that everyone is on the same page. An outside cleaning company will often include a checklist of what the contract covers. But if you outsource all of your cleaning, don't just rely on the company's list; make sure that you add anything you feel is important before signing the contract.

Here is a sample cleaning checklist, but see part II, "Tools," for a more detailed breakdown:

Daily
- Disinfect all touch surfaces (toilet and sink handles, doorknobs, light switches—anything patrons and staff touch daily). This helps keep germs and sickness at bay.
- Clean and disinfect all fixtures in restrooms, and if possible, refresh the restrooms while the library is open.
- Clean and disinfect kitchen fixtures and appliances.
- Wipe off any spots on the surfaces of tables, desks, counters, and so on.
- Wipe off fingerprints and smudges on glass doors, windows, and partitions.
- Wet mop floors in restrooms, main tile areas, the kitchen, and entranceways, especially in the winter and spring months.
- Vacuum the main carpeted areas for debris and dirt.
- Empty all trash receptacles.

Weekly
- Thoroughly mop and vacuum all the floors and carpets and spot clean any stains on the carpets.
- Wipe down all the interior windows to remove any dust or debris.
- Wipe down window sills and desk/tabletop surfaces.
- Inspect any upholstered furniture for stains and all furniture for damage.

Monthly

- Dust shelving and the high surfaces in the library (tops of shelves, air ducts/vents, etc.) and eliminate any cobwebs that have formed during the month.
- Clean out the break room refrigerator (and any others that may be in the building), discarding any undated food and wiping all interior surfaces.

Quarterly/semiannually

- Deep clean carpet, tile, or other flooring. (Many libraries have their floors deep cleaned on a regular basis, either all of the flooring at one time or in sections, depending on the building's size.)
- Fully clean all windows, inside and out.
- Clean the upholstery of heavily used furniture.

Whether you are using library staff or an outside vendor for cleaning, performing either monthly or quarterly walkthroughs of your building is critical to ensuring the building stays clean. Most outside cleaning vendors work at night after the library is closed and may not be able to see as well as someone working in the daylight. Having cleaners come every so often during the day can help keep spots from being overlooked. You might also find it helpful to take and share pictures of problem areas during the month, either via e-mail or during your walk-around so that the vendor or your staff can see exactly what you expect. Taking pictures of how you would like an area to look is also helpful in creating a clear visual for what you expect to see each day.

MAINTENANCE OF FACILITY AND GROUNDS

As part of the walk-through to ensure that the building is clean, you and/or your maintenance person should be observing any maintenance issues that have arisen. Check around toilets, sinks, and any other place where water can leak. Look for potential current and future issues.

On a weekly basis, you and/or your maintenance person should note any lighting issues, inside and out, and replace any burned-out bulbs. Some lights may require a ladder or lift to reach them to replace bulbs, or they may need to have their ballasts changed. If the library does not have the staff or equipment to perform these duties, an outside vendor may be necessary. If the task can wait until more lights are out, then keep a running list of the lights that need to be replaced until there is enough work to warrant contacting an electrician. Hiring an electrician can be expensive, but it's worth it if you don't have the equipment or knowledge to repair lighting on your own. Hiring a professional often pays for itself in the long run. If you have security cameras, make sure they are all working correctly too. They provide peace of mind but do no good if they are not in working order.

On a monthly basis, inspect all your doors to ensure they are in working order. Do they lock and unlock easily? Staff should not have to struggle to lock or unlock a door. The mechanisms inside are meant to work easily, but over time and after many uses, the internal parts may wear out and need to be replaced. Also check the alarms on the emergency exit doors. Most of these doors are alarmed, and those alarms may be battery operated. Make sure the batteries are charged and in working order.

As mentioned earlier, your vendors (e.g., for HVAC, alarm, fire suppression, and water systems) should perform inspections and maintenance checks at least annually, but preferably semiannually, on all your facility systems to ensure they are in proper working order. This will also allow them to check for potential issues and suggest a plan in the event of a large expenditure in the library's future. Set up a schedule to check the seals around your windows and doors to ensure that the caulk is air/watertight. This will prevent weather and animal damage. Check with your municipality about its requirements for inspections. The municipality may require its own inspections in additions to those performed by your vendors. Fire departments are especially conscious of their public buildings and want to ensure the safest places possible for the residents of their communities.

Your facility will likely have outside space, with grass, possibly shrubs and flowers, and certainly sidewalks and parking lots. You can hire vendors to mow the lawn, maintain the flowers and shrubs, and perform snow removal and salting of your lots. Depending on your location, your exterior site maintenance budget will vary and you must prepare for the what-ifs of weather uncertainty.

The spring and fall are good times to inspect all outdoor aspects of your building:

Landscaping

- Are the trees and shrubs as healthy as they should be?
- Does anything need to be removed and/or replaced?
- Is the mulch fresh and doing its job?
- Are tree roots popping out of the ground?
- Does the lawn have bare patches that need to be reseeded/resodded?
- Are gutters and downspouts clear and in working order?

Parking lot and walkways

- Are there potholes or large cracks in the parking lot?
- Are the parking stripes visible and are the parking bumpers in the proper place and in good repair?
- Are the walkways even and free from large cracks or crevices that could be a tripping hazard?

Once a year, generally at the beginning of your budget cycle, you need to determine if any facility or grounds improvements may be necessary in the coming year. Check your capital improvement plan (discussed in the next section) for any upcoming improvements, but also take the time to determine what may need to be added to the plan. By being vigilant as to any potential repairs or improvements, you will be able to budget accordingly in the next few years.

There are always times when things break without notice, even with careful regular inspections, but by being consistent and thorough, you will minimize those events. In order to be prepared when larger improvements, repairs, or replacements are necessary, it is a good practice to have a capital improvement plan.

CAPITAL IMPROVEMENT PLAN

Whether you have a new facility or an older one, having a capital improvement plan is a necessity. This document is a short-range plan, usually four to ten years (but can expand out to twenty years in some instances), that identifies capital projects and equipment purchases, provides a planning schedule and a comprehensive listing of all the mechanical systems, and identifies options for financing the plan. The capital improvement plan should be linked to the library's annual budget and likely the library's strategic plan. Depending on the library and community, this plan may be a short spreadsheet or a large multipage document.

Regardless of the size of the library, the plan should include at least the following items:

Facility interior
- Painted surfaces
- Carpet
- Tile
- Surfaces that have wall covering
- Special features that need attention

Facility exterior
- Brick walls
- Windows
- Skylights (if applicable)
- Doors
- Parking lot
- Walkways
- Vegetation
- Roof

Mechanical equipment
- HVAC units
- Water heaters

- Fire alarms
- Mechanical doors

IT equipment
- Server(s)
- Routers
- Uninterrupted power source
- Desktop computers
- Laptops
- Wireless access points
- Security cameras

Other equipment
- Printers
- Copiers
- Laminator
- Typewriter

Furniture/fixtures—interior
- Seating for patrons and staff
- Tables/desks for patrons and staff
- Shelving
- Lighting and special lighting
- Toilets
- Sinks
- Refrigerator
- Microwave/toaster oven

Furniture/fixtures—exterior
- Benches/tables
- Parking lot lights
- Library signage (electronic, fixed)
- Special features (water fountain, sculptures, etc.)

When putting together this list, you want to provide information on what you currently have in addition to a cost estimate for what you will need down the road. Each item has an average life expectancy, and that is one of the most critical pieces of information because it helps you predict how long before a major piece of equipment will fail, allowing you to put away money every year in an effort to avoid taking on debt.

If you have a new facility, the architect may have created this document and included it as part of the final documents received. If you are in the process of building a new facility, ask the architect to create this for you. If you are working at an older facility, a professional appraisal of the facility and grounds may be a good starting point for creating a capital improvement plan. While you may want to do all of this on your own, at some point you will need to bring in someone who can give you cost estimates for these projects. However, you can start by gathering most of this information yourself or having your maintenance person gather it. When gathering information, be sure to research any new laws or trends that are facility specific, including complying with the ADA, providing gender-neutral restrooms, or offering private rooms for employees who are nursing.

Once you have gathered all the necessary information, create another column in your document to list replacement costs. You will need to do some research on the costs for replacing the items, and you will have to make concessions for inflation when projecting out a number of years, but even if you are not exact, having reasonable figures in this column will help you calculate what the library may need in any given year for facility improvements. This will help determine the library's financial needs in the short term and the long term. Be sure to add or delete items as you add or remove items (e.g., equipment) from the library.

Now that you have a completed capital improvement plan, use it. This document should be consulted whenever you are planning larger projects as well as during your annual budget planning.

EXAMPLES OF INFORMATION TO GATHER FOR CAPITAL IMPROVEMENT PLAN

- **Equipment:** model name and number, manufacturer, cost new, and life expectancy
- **Furniture, interior and exterior:** model name and number (if applicable), manufacturer, cost new, life expectancy, and fabric name/color
- **Fixtures:** same as furniture
- **Walls, painted:** paint manufacturer (e.g., Sherwin-Williams), color name and/or number, sheen (e.g., eggshell, flat), and date painted
- **Walls, covered:** covering manufacturer, color name and/or number, date installed, and life expectancy
- **Carpet:** manufacturer, color name and/or number, cost new, life expectancy, and date installed
- **Tile:** manufacturer, color name and/or number, cost new, life expectancy, and date installed
- **Parking lot walkways:** type of material (e.g., concrete, asphalt, stone), cost new, date installed

⚙ REVIEW AND REFLECT

KEY TAKEAWAYS

Buildings are your largest asset, and you need to take time to get to know the different systems and processes inside and out.

Common building systems you should know are these:

- HVAC
- Electrical
- Plumbing
- Fire suppression

Have a plan for cleaning and maintaining your facility and grounds, including scheduling regular maintenance and inspections.

Systems can be quite expensive, so having a capital improvement plan for upgrades and repairs ensures you are not caught unprepared.

SELF-CHECK

- What vendors do we contract with for maintenance work?
- How is the cleaning handled for our building?
- Do we have checklists in place for maintaining our building?
- What building systems are in place and where are they located?
- Who does the work on our building, inside and outside?
- Where is our vendor contact list?
- Where are the library's blueprints?

QUESTIONS FOR REFLECTION

- What maintenance systems do I need to know about immediately?
- What do I need to know in terms of building maintenance if there is an emergency today?
- Whom can I contact to help me learn?

ADDITIONAL RESOURCES

See part II for this additional resource on buildings:

- Sample 8.1: Library Cleaning Checklist

⬇ **Download a CAPTIAL IMPROVEMENT PLAN and MAINTENANCE CHECKLIST on our website at www.librarydirectorstoolkit.com/resources.**

Barclay, D. A., and E. Scott. *The Library Renovation, Maintenance, and Construction Handbook.* New York: Neal-Schuman, 2011.

Piotrowicz, L., and S. Osgood. *Building Science 101: A Primer for Librarians.* Chicago: ALA Editions, 2010.

Schlipf, F., and J. A. Moorman. *Practical Handbook of Library Architecture: Creating Spaces That Work.* Chicago: ALA Editions, 2018.

9

EMERGENCY PLANNING

After reading this chapter, you will know the following:

- The importance of an emergency plan and how to create one specific to your library
- How to create an emergency contact list
- How to implement an emergency plan
- How to maintain minimum ongoing operations after a disaster
- How to train staff on emergency procedures

As with using an attorney, emergency planning is something you hope never to have to worry about, but in the event of an emergency, having a plan in place is necessary. As the library director, you are responsible for the well-being of thousands of people (staff and public) and a facility that houses not only these people but also the library's materials, furniture, and equipment.

Emergency planning encompasses many things. In the event of a fire, natural disaster, or lockdown, you need to have an evacuation or a shelter-in-place plan for staff and patrons. The library should have a procedure manual on how to handle emergencies that is available to all staff. This manual should include the following:

- Emergency contacts for staff and building vendors
- Instructions on how to deal with different types of emergencies
- Building maps with evacuation routes and safety areas marked
- Emergency communication plan
- Technology backup and recovery instructions

- Information on how to handle minimal operations, including staffing
  and payroll, in the event of a long-term shutdown

It is important for all staff to know what the emergency plan is and to receive continuous training on responses to emergency situations. If an emergency does happen, having a clear action plan will be key for handling situations successfully.

PLANNING FOR AN EMERGENCY

Think of every possible emergency scenario that could happen for your library. Start with the most serious concerns that could affect the building and anything specific to your geographic location, such as fire, tornado, hurricane, flooding, earthquake, and so on. Then think of people-related concerns, like disruptive patrons, fighting, active threats, and so forth. The following sample list will help you get started:

Environment
- Fire
- Flood
- Tornado
- Hurricane
- Earthquake

Building
- Elevator entrapment
- Power outage
- Vandalism
- System (HVAC, water, sewer, etc.) malfunction

Human
- Irate/angry patron
- Irate/angry staff member
- Unattended/missing child
- Disruptive person
- Physical altercations between patrons and/or staff
- Patrons with mental or physical disabilities who request accommodations
- Rioting
- Active threat/violent intruder

Your manual will need procedures for dealing with each such event as well as for other situations that may be specific to your community or library. Many of these events will require similar procedures, but you should still have an evacuation (or shelter-in-place) plan for each.

EMERGENCY EVACUATION PLANS

Start with a map of the library and surrounding grounds. Mark the emergency exits throughout the entire building and determine the best routes of egress to those doors. Remember that emergency exits are just that—doors that can be exited from by pushing outward without having to overcome barriers (moving furniture, unlocking with keys or codes, etc.). You should have the fire or emergency services department for your community perform regular inspections of the building and grounds to ensure that all doors and emergency exits are safe and appropriate for entering and exiting. If this has not taken place or is not happening on a regular basis, contact the appropriate department and request an inspection.

Next, on the map, divide the library into zones based on each emergency exit. This will delineate how people should exit the building based on where they are located in the building. Draw the evacuation routes. Designate a meeting area (or areas) outside the building that is far enough away for all people to be safe from any potential harm (e.g., fire, explosion) but close enough for everyone to get to the meeting place safely and with little help. This place should be away from where emergency vehicles will need to be for access to the building. Be sure the area is posted with appropriate signage.

Once you have created this initial evacuation map, go back and map out alternate evacuation routes in the event that one or more of the previously designated exits are blocked by fire, fallen debris, and so forth. Preplanning and having multiple evacuation routes will save lives in the event of an emergency.

You should also prepare for an emergency that will require people to stay inside the building. The first step is to determine the safest place for people to congregate. For a tornado, an interior room with no windows is best. For a general lockdown to prevent anyone from entering the building, the meeting room might suffice. An active threat may require that all doors be locked and barred, which means people would be in different areas. Contact your local emergency services department to discuss these issues and ask for recommendations for each scenario. Create a map for each type of shelter-in-place incident.

Once you have completed the different evacuation maps, create a list of procedures for each emergency issue. These procedures should cover the entire process from how people are notified of the emergency through each step until the emergency is concluded. Use these questions to guide your planning:

- What should each step include?
- What should patrons do?
- Where should patrons go?
- Who is going to make patrons aware of the problem and/or guide them in the process?
- What should staff be doing?
- Should staff be the ones to help patrons or secure safety on their own?

- How should people be accounted for once everyone has met up?
- Who is in charge per shift?

Write it all down.

EMERGENCY CONTACT LIST

An integral part of an emergency manual is the contact list. This list should include, at minimum, contact information for the following:

- Board of trustees
- Staff
- Key village/city staff
- Emergency vendor services (e.g., plumbing, electric, HVAC, board-up companies)
- Insurance company claims line (including policy numbers)
- Library attorney
- Utility contractors (including account numbers)
- Local media
- Delivery vendors (U.S. Post Office, UPS, FedEx, etc.)
- Technology staff for library (in-house staff or outsourced vendor)
- ILS contacts
- Library system/state library
- Materials' vendors
- Neighboring libraries (to ask if they can help serve patrons' needs)

It should also include this information:

- How to log on to website and social media accounts
- Technology backup plan (more on this later)
- HR and payroll (vendor contact, if applicable)

EXAMPLE EMERGENCY SCENARIO: FIRE

Let's run through a standard emergency: fire.

The fire alarm has gone off and there is obvious smoke. No one knows where the fire is, but given the smoke, the likelihood of a fire is great. There are eight staff, including the library director and two managers, placed throughout the building with twenty-three patrons inside. Eight are at computers, three are in the adult stacks, and the rest are attending a children's storytime in the youth department.

We have all been trained since grade school that everyone needs to evacuate when a fire alarm goes off, so everyone should and will leave the building without being told, right? Ideally, yes, but past experience has taught us that this is not always the case. It is likely that the parents and children will evacuate quickly; their main concern will be the well-being of the children, so they will likely leave through the front entrance or an emergency door located close to where they are. The patrons in the stacks will hopefully leave via the closest exit. Ideally, the people at the computers will leave promptly as well, but often they don't want to leave their work unfinished.

Staff members should not be required to do anything but save themselves in the event of an emergency. This should be explicitly stated in the emergency manual and in all emergency training. However, many may feel it is their moral and ethical obligation to make sure everyone is safe. If it is safe to do so, staff may stay back to make sure that all people are evacuating to the nearest exit. Each department should have its own zone to clear, including checking stacks, seating, study rooms, and restrooms. Staff should be aware of who is in the building during the day and should pay attention once everyone has evacuated to ensure no one is missing. Make sure the building is cleared. Everyone should meet at the designated meeting place, allowing the firemen and other emergency responders to perform their duties.

Depending on the size of the library, it may or may not be easy to determine if everyone is safely outside. Be sure to communicate as much as possible with staff to determine whether all areas have been cleared, and let the emergency team know so they can look for any missing people in the building. At this point, let's assume everyone is safe. The responders put out the fire and indicate that the building is unsafe and needs to be closed.

This scenario should give enough details to enable crafting the related emergency procedures, including designating who is responsible for what. Remember that an emergency can happen at any time, and Murphy's Law suggests it will happen when no manager is on duty or the director is out of town on vacation and unreachable. Be sure to account for such possibilities in your procedure planning.

Once you have crafted the procedures for the list of various emergencies, have library staff review them and offer input. Once the procedures have been vetted by staff, have the appropriate emergency personnel in town (fire, police, etc.) review the procedures and then walk through your building to see if they have any additional thoughts or recommendations for improvement.

Now that all the evacuation/shelter-in-place procedures have been vetted, you are a third of the way finished. Let's go back to the fire emergency scenario.

RECOVERING FROM AN EMERGENCY

In the earlier fire emergency scenario, the fire department deemed that the library was unsafe and so is not able to reopen due to fire, smoke, and water damage. Thus, a procedure for what to do after an emergency is necessary. As with all emergencies, the after response will be as varied as the initial response. In the instance of a fire, the following will need to be accomplished immediately:

1. *Designate a communications and media point person.* Someone has to be the media point person to communicate with the board, staff, village/city officials, and patrons about the fire. This person will also need to coordinate updates to the library website and other social media outlets so that everyone knows what has happened and what it will mean for library services. The local media may get involved, and having one point person ensures that there is one message from the library. Depending on the size of the library, the point person may be the director, assistant director, or public relations person. This person should be in action during the event to help organize the chaos.

2. *Contact the library insurance company.* All insurance companies have a twenty-four-hour emergency claims hotline. Once contacted, your insurance company should dispatch someone immediately or, at the very least, give instruction on the next steps. If the company dispatches someone immediately, that representative may take care of the next steps for the library as part of the claims process. It is important to know exactly what will happen in the event of a claim, so be sure to ask your insurance carrier before any actual emergency happens.

3. *Secure the building.* All utilities need to be shut off, and all openings need to be boarded up. Doors and windows that are intact should be secured and locked. The library must be protected from the elements, animals, and vandals. The insurance company may take care of this as part of the claim, or library personnel may need to call the utility companies and board-up services or a combination of both.

4. *Begin remediation of damaged surfaces and library materials and furniture.* Response time is critical in the wake of damage, especially when water is involved. Mold can start to form within twenty-four hours of water exposure. The insurance company will likely start whatever remediation process is necessary right away as part of the claim. The company will take an inventory of damaged items and surfaces and call in its panel of preferred vendors to remove items, dry surfaces, and whatever else is necessary to take care of the physical building, furnishings, and collection. If this is not part of the insurance company's claims process, the library should have the necessary vendor information available in the emergency manual so the process can begin right away.

These steps will be necessary for any major emergency that involves the building, but other steps may be necessary depending on the emergency. All steps need to be documented in the emergency manual so that everyone knows what procedures to follow after an incident. All possible scenarios should be included in the emergency manual along with the procedures and details for addressing each of them.

LIBRARY APPRAISAL AND INVENTORY

The library should have had an appraisal done at some point to determine the insured value of all contents. This may have been done by the insurance company as part of determining the library's coverage or by an independent agency. This appraisal, which should also be included in the emergency manual, will contain all contents of the building, from collections and furniture to equipment and technology components. Having a handy list of all contents will help in identifying damage and in formulating a repair/replacement plan. While typically this will be an electronic document, database, or spreadsheet, you still should have an off-site backup, either electronic or printed out, somewhere that is easily accessible.

LIBRARY COLLECTIONS, FURNITURE, AND ELECTRONICS

What happens to the library collections when damaged? Can the furniture be saved? And what about all the library data that was once in the now-ruined server? These possibilities all have to be planned for and managed. Depending on damage and response time, you may be able to save these items, but if you can't, you need to have a plan in place. It will be easy enough to replace materials and furniture when the time presents itself. The most critical of these issues is the technology.

Libraries depend on having data available, and many will have in-house servers to house staff and patron data. All libraries should have a data backup plan in place, whether it is as simple as downloading all the server contents to an external drive weekly (and keeping that drive off-site) or backing up data in the cloud daily. The upside of technology is that virtually anything can be accomplished that once had to be done in person or via telephone. Data can be readily available in small and varied formats. The downside is we are very dependent on technology and may take it for granted. The key is to make sure the library has a formal backup procedure in place and follows it on a regular basis.

EXTENDED EMERGENCY CLOSURES

If the library has to be closed for an extended period of time (three or more days), you will need to make some decisions. Does the library continue to provide services? If so, what services will be provided and what will that look like?

The library board (and director) will need to hold an emergency meeting to determine the extent of the damage, assess what services can be continued, and decide for what length of time and where they can be continued. The services may be a minimum of online reference that staff can do from home or something more extensive in another location. Perhaps there is a storefront available for the library to rent or available space in the village hall or community center.

COMMUNITY-WIDE EMERGENCIES

In the event of a community-wide disaster (earthquake, tornado, flooding, etc.), the library may be the only place where the community has access to Internet, computers, and service providers. If the library is physically able to be open in a safe and limited way, this may be a good idea. If the library can relocate some services to a temporary location to meet the needs of the community, this would be optimal. If it is at all possible, maintaining some sort of library presence, even on the library website or via social media, is a good idea.

STAFFING DURING AND AFTER EMERGENCIES

Whether the library closes for a few days or a few months, one of the major decisions the board and director need to make is what to do with staff. If the library is closed and no staff members are working, do they continue to get paid? The library director and likely any management staff will be working through the disaster, and they will need to be paid. Personnel decisions are critical during an emergency. These include not only the decision about utilizing staff and paying them but also determining how to pay them if the library does not have the ability to cut checks or process payroll. Delineating a plan to continue payroll is necessary, and this plan should be included in the emergency manual. Be careful not to include any sensitive personal information, like Social Security numbers and birthdates, in the manual.

IMPLEMENTATION AND TRAINING

Now that the emergency manual has been written, every scenario and subsequent procedure has been thought of and detailed, there is still one more thing to do. You must communicate the details of the plans to the staff and board. Continuous staff training on the evacuation/shelter-in-place procedures, and all the other aspects of the emergency planning, is necessary. Training is integral to a successful emergency plan. Not only should staff read the manual; they need to know it. They must practice all the scenarios without opening the manual in order to feel comfortable executing the procedures during an emergency.

Staff should practice, practice, practice as often as possible. Bring in the fire department to show staff how to use a fire extinguisher and run the evacuation plan. Have the police or other law enforcement work with the staff on how to respond during an active threat incident. Be sure they are trained on how to manage the patrons in these instances to help ensure patron safety as well.

Be sure to keep the manual and procedures updated. Review the manual every six months or once a year to make sure the contact numbers are still correct and that the procedures will still work in light of any recent changes. Managers should be part of this process and have the pertinent professionals reevaluate the changes to ensure they are in compliance with their needs as well.

Any new staff need to be trained on emergency procedures. This should be part of the onboarding of new staff. Managers should run through the procedures with new staff since there will likely be department duties for an evacuation or shelter-in-place situation. This will also help to reinforce the procedures for the managers.

✿ REVIEW AND REFLECT

KEY TAKEAWAYS

Libraries need to be prepared in the event of an emergency. Ensuring the safety of staff and the public is contingent on having well-thought-out plans.

Your written emergency plan should contain all possible emergency scenarios and a map of all evacuation routes. This map should be posted in the building for inspection by staff and patrons.

Create an emergency contact list that includes key people from the library, vendors, and community.

Once an emergency occurs, the library must find a way to function and assign the tasks that need to be performed to different people.

To ensure that planning and operations will go smoothly, all staff need to be fully trained on a regular basis.

SELF-CHECK

- Does the library have an emergency manual or, at minimum, some emergency planning documents?
- Do I have a hard copy of our emergency plan at home with contact information?
- What will our insurance company do in the event of a claim?
- Is our electronic data backed up? If so, where and how often?
- Have staff been trained on how to handle emergencies?

QUESTIONS FOR REFLECTION

- What specifics should I include in the emergency plan?
- How detailed do I need to make the emergency plan?
- What training do I need to set up for staff?
- Who should be responsible for training new staff on emergency procedures?

ADDITIONAL RESOURCES

See part II for this additional resource on sample emergency procedures:

- Sample 9.1: Staff Emergency Responses

⤓ **Download additional resources on our website at www.librarydirectorstoolkit.com/resources.**

Albrecht, S. *Library Security: Better Communication, Safer Facilities.* Chicago: ALA Editions, 2015.

American Library Association. "Disaster Preparedness and Recovery." www.ala.org/advocacy/govinfo/disasterpreparedness.

Graham, W. *The Black Belt Librarian: Real-World Safety and Security.* Chicago: ALA Editions, 2012.

Halsted, D., S. Clifton, and D. Wilson. *Library as Safe Haven: Disaster Planning, Response, and Recovery: A How-To-Do-It Manual for Librarians.* Chicago: ALA Neal-Schuman, 2014.

10

TECHNOLOGY

After reading this chapter, you will know the following:

- ◼ How to determine the technology your library needs
- ◼ How to put together an IT budget and technology replacement plan
- ◼ How to provide the level of IT support your library needs
- ◼ How to set and enforce technology competencies for staff
- ◼ How to stay current on technology issues and trends

Y ou may shake your head, thinking that technology is already incorporated into libraries and this is now a nonissue, but technology has been increasing in library budgets for years and shows no signs of slowing down. As the library director, you need to ensure that your library is up-to-date and providing your patrons with the core services they require in regard to technology.

The library director sets the tone for how technology will be regarded in the library. Libraries are uniquely situated to be able to help patrons become comfortable with technology. But to do that, we have to be comfortable with it ourselves. Where do you even begin?

TECHNOLOGY ASSESSMENT

First, start with what you need. Gain an understanding of what is currently in place. If you are in luck, you will have a great technology replacement plan and be completely up-to-date.

To get a handle on things, sit down with your IT manager or IT support staff to get an understanding of what your library has in place. If you are the IT manager, reach out to the vendors that you purchase IT support from and ask them to assist you in understanding your system. You could also seek advice from a local school, municipality, or library system; it's possible one of these will have someone on staff who can sit down with you and explain how the technology in your library is set up.

The following are some questions to ask IT staff or vendors:

- Does the library have a technology replacement plan?
- Is there an inventory of all devices and equipment?
- Is there an inventory of all software and licenses, purchase dates, costs, and expiration dates of licenses?
- What documentation is there of all systems and infrastructure?
- How does the infrastructure work (or how is it set up)?
- Is there regular maintenance and backup of data?
- If backup takes place, is it done on-site, off-site, or in the cloud?
- How are technology issues and requests tracked?
- What are the library's most common issues or requests?
- What, if anything, is recommended to make our system stronger for our staff and patrons?
- Is the library adequately protected from cyberattacks?
- What training do we do to keep up with current IT practices?
- Do we work with any outside vendors on IT projects?
- Who handles the support for our ILS?

Once you have the basic framework of what is in place at the library, determine what might be missing. Here are some core items to have:

- Telephone
- Voice mail and/or answering machine
- Fax and/or scanner
- Photocopier
- Internet access, for both the staff and the public
- E-mail accounts for all staff and a minimum of one e-mail account for the board
- Website
- Computers
- Printers
- Antivirus protection
- Basic computer software
- ILS

The following things are nice to have but, depending on library size and budget, may not be possible or necessary:

- Wireless access (Wi-Fi)
- Networking (local versus wide area)
- Library intranet
- Self-checkout machines
- Social media accounts for the library
- Tablets and e-readers for checkout
- Projector, screen, and other technology for meeting rooms
- Adaptive technologies for patrons with disabilities
- Server backups
- Backup Internet

Talking to professional IT staff helps you to understand the core services and infrastructure to have in place. Making a list of what is needed versus what is currently in place will help you prioritize actions to take based on your budget, the critical nature of the current environment, and the timeline to complete.

CREATING A TECHNOLOGY PLAN

Once you have completed the technology assessment, create a written technology plan. Part of creating that plan is listing every piece of equipment and licensing that will need to be replaced. List the current cost for replacing each item and the expected date of replacement. This list now becomes the core of the technology replacement plan, showing when equipment will need to be replaced and the associated costs. This plan is not unlike the library's capital improvement plan, but for technology. The key to creating a usable plan is to include everything in it. Don't make the assumption that equipment will last forever because it is expensive. Everything fails, and having a plan in place allows you to be proactive instead of reactive.

Once you have an itemized list of technology equipment, evaluate it annually. When reviewing the plan, if you find that some equipment that is due for replacement is working fine and does not need to be replaced, note this on the list. If it is still functional and the budget money can be spent elsewhere, that is fine; just remember to account for the replacement in future budgeting.

Now that there is a replacement plan in place, make a list of your annual IT costs. These are the things that are renewed each year, like database licensing renewals, and so forth. Not sure what these costs are? Look at the bills over the past few years to get a sense of what came out of the technology budget lines. Some items may renew for multiple years to garner cost savings (websites, domain names, etc.), so be sure to go back a few years. This will indicate how much has been spent for web hosting, antivirus protection, and so on. Make a list of the costs for each of these categories, as these are fixed costs and will likely remain the same each year.

Unlike other budgets, which can be estimated pretty closely to what is needed in funding for the next year, technology budgets can be trickier. For example, that planned upgrade to the phone system turns into a replacement of the entire phone system because the old system became obsolete; or while planning the upgrade to the servers, it is discovered that the switches are more than a dozen years old and need to be replaced too. Anything can happen when it comes to new and upgraded technology, so it is best to be prepared for any possibility.

When creating an IT budget, it is best to start with what is known:

- What pieces of hardware need to be replaced or upgraded?
- What software will need to be purchased or upgraded?
- What are the base costs for technology (ILS, server maintenance, etc.)?
- What IT projects are planned for the coming year and what is the approximate cost of each? (Not sure of the cost of a project? Try asking other libraries, or go straight to a few IT firms and get quotes on what a project may cost.)

When budgeting for IT, add in a contingency cost for every project. We recommend adding 10 percent to the estimate for your contingency cost. After the budget numbers are calculated, add in a little more money, if it's feasible. A project may pop up, or the library might decide to try some newer technology. Having a small contingency fund will enable the library to move forward with these and not wait until the next fiscal year. How much to put aside will depend on the library. For small libraries it might be $500, while for larger libraries it might be $10,000. The amount is going to depend on your other budget costs, type of community, and the comfort level of the board.

IT STAFFING

Setting a budget may seem easy compared to determining how to provide IT support to the library. Hiring for the IT department can be one of the most challenging aspects to being a director. For most directors, this is the position with which they have the least familiarity and which can cause the most damage. Having competent IT support for the library is not a luxury, but a necessity.

There are different ways you can opt to provide support to the library:

- Employ dedicated on-site IT staff.
- Outsource IT support to an outside company that will provide IT support either in person or remotely.
- Have library vendors provide support.
- Use a combination of the previous options.

DEDICATED ON-SITE IT STAFF

Many libraries choose not to outsource any services and prefer to hire everything from janitorial staff to IT support. The advantage to this is that the director can choose people who are a good fit for the library. Hiring someone to manage your IT support as a member of your staff means that the person can also easily be woven into the other work you do, attend manager meetings, and be a part of the staff.

Depending on many factors, hiring your IT staff may be the more financially responsible solution. However, this depends on your geographic region, budget, availability of skilled staff, and availability of outside vendors to provide support. While it may be less expensive, having an in-house IT staff depends on many factors and should be carefully evaluated.

The downside to having in-house IT support is that that person(s) will not be an expert in every type of technology. The other downside is that you don't have others to provide a second opinion. If the IT staffer tells you that this is what needs to happen, you don't have anyone else to tell you whether this is the best route to take.

OUTSOURCED IT SUPPORT

With an IT firm, there is the full knowledge of an entire company to call on for support. Hiring an outside IT company to handle the library's IT support means that you usually have access to staff who specialize in different areas and can be called upon to help when you have specific issues with phones, servers, and so on. Outside vendors, depending on the company hired, can also give a big-picture view of IT support and put together a plan for providing help. They can educate the library staff on best practices and provide warnings about potential security risks. Depending on the size and budget of your library and the level of support you wish to receive, outsourcing may make more or less fiscal sense.

One downside may be that an outside vendor won't be committed to your library in the same way that staff are and will typically not attend some of the non-IT meetings that on-site staff would. This means they are not as attuned to the library and not as aware of library-related issues. They might serve other nonlibrary clients and not know about the particular quirks that come with helping libraries with their IT, like managing an ILS or providing patron IT support as well as staff IT support.

If your library does decide to hire outside IT support, be sure to vet the companies; ask if they serve other libraries, and call those libraries for references.

VENDOR IT SUPPORT

Sometimes hiring an outside firm is not possible or feasible, but there is no expertise in house to handle the needed IT support. Looking at the vendors that the library has purchased hardware and software from may provide a starting point for achieving an interim level of support for the library. Many vendors (like Microsoft, Dell, HP, etc.) offer care packages that include a call-in service for clients to receive phone support. This can be more cost-effective, depending on the service plan you purchase.

The downside to this type of support is that no one is looking out for the library's long-term technology needs. The vendors are solving only the short-term problems that arise and are not on-site to deal with the day-to-day issues.

This type of support is recommended if it is not possible to hire anyone to provide support and all IT support is falling to the library director or other staff members whose primary job and area of expertise are not in IT. This level of support is better than nothing, but it won't help with ensuring a strong technology platform today and in the future.

COMBO PACKAGE

Another option is to not pick just one route, but to choose a route that best fits the needs of the library. Perhaps that means having an IT firm do large projects while an on-site staff member handles day-to-day issues. Another option is to purchase support packages for the hardware and software vendors but have those managed by an outside vendor or staff person. There are untold combinations for IT support. Determining what is best for your library means understanding your library's needs. Ask questions to ascertain what will work best at your library:

- What types of questions are asked on a daily basis by staff and patrons?
- What level of support is needed for system maintenance?
- How much money is needed for support?
- Which vendors offer support with their products?
- What is the current state of technology in our library?

There is no one right or wrong way to provide IT support. The key is to determine what the library's needs are and to plan accordingly based on budget and the services available in the area.

TECHNOLOGY COMPETENCIES

Now that you have a plan in place for the library's technology needs, including creating a budget and providing IT support, how do you ensure that staff are on board? Library staff members don't need to be well versed on all aspects of technology, but they should be comfortable with basic technology tasks. An easy barometer is to ask, "What do we expect most patrons to be able to do on their own?" If you expect patrons to be able to do it, staff should be able to as well. Ideally, most staff should be able to do some intermediate tasks, and some may have more advanced skills. Technology changes too fast for anyone to stay an expert for too long without making an effort to remain current.

Technology competencies provide a framework for staff to understand the technology expectations you have for them. There are many categories to focus on when thinking about technology competencies, but most fall into several categories on the front end and back end of the work that staff members do. When thinking of competencies for public-facing tasks, ask yourself, "Do I expect a typical patron to be able to do this on his or her own?" If your answer is yes, then staff should also be expected to be able to do that task. Here are some basics that staff at most libraries will need to know:

Telephone
- Answer a call.
- Transfer a call.
- Hold/park a call.
- Set up voice mail.
- Check voice mail.
- Find names and phone numbers in the directory.

Copier
- Make a single-sided copy.
- Make a double-sided copy.
- Reduce a copy.
- Enlarge a copy.
- Collate copies.
- Staple copies.
- Make copies with special paper using the bypass tray.

E-mail
- Send an e-mail to an individual.
- Send an e-mail to a group/department.
- Send an e-mail with an attachment.
- Open an e-mail with an attachment.
- Forward an e-mail.
- Reply to an individual e-mail.
- Reply to a group e-mail.
- Search for previously sent or received messages.
- Set an automatic away message to reply to incoming e-mail.

General technology
- Understand what a monitor is and how to turn it off and on.
- Understand what a computer processing unit (CPU) is, how the monitor connects to it, and how to turn it off and on.
- Understand what a mouse is and how it connects to the CPU.

- Understand what a keyboard is, how it connects to the computer, and what the function keys are and how to use them.
- Understand where the printers are and how to select different printers for printing.
- Know what a flash drive is and how to save something to a flash drive.
- Understand the Windows operating system, its desktop, and its icons and how to navigate through and use them.
- Manage files and folders: know the different folders on the shared drive and where to find items; know how to change the name of a file or folder and how to move it.
- Search for files or folders.
- Understand functions common to most applications, such as copy, paste, open, save, and print.
- Adjust screen resolution.
- Print all or part of a document.
- Know how to use basic shortcuts (e.g., cut, copy, paste) with either a mouse or the keyboard.
- Understand mouse scrolling.
- Use Task Manager to close unresponsive programs.
- Log on and off a computer.
- Perform screen shots.
- Send a fax.
- Scan a document.

Microsoft Office

- Open a document.
- Create a Microsoft Word document.
- Create a Microsoft Excel spreadsheet.
- Create a PowerPoint presentation.
- Create a flyer in Microsoft Publisher.
- Copy/paste.
- Save files in various places.
- Print and adjust printed pages.
- Convert a document to PDF.

Integrated library system (ILS)

- Know how to use equipment related to circulation, cataloging, and the ILS, including self-checkout machines, receipt printers, and bar code scanners.
- Check the status of an item.
- Search the catalog.

■ Place a hold in the OPAC (online public access catalog).
■ Place a hold on the staff module of the ILS.
■ Renew an item in the OPAC.
■ Renew an item on the staff module of the ILS.
■ Add a new patron.
■ Update a patron record.
■ Mark an item missing, damaged, and so forth.
■ Update an item record.
■ View items on hold in the OPAC.
■ Perform an advanced search using limiters.
■ Withdraw an item.
■ Add an item to the catalog.

Downloadables
■ Search for an item.
■ Place a hold.
■ Set up a new account.
■ Check out an e-book, e-audiobook, e-magazine, e-video, and so forth.
■ Download an e-book (computer).
■ Download an e-book (device).
■ Download an e-book (tablet/smartphone).
■ Return an e-book early.
■ Check out an audiobook.
■ Download an audiobook (computer).
■ Download an audiobook (tablet/smartphone).

Payroll (if automated)
■ Log in and look at your timecard.
■ Submit a time-off request.
■ Look at your accruals.

Computer reservation and print management
■ Log on to a patron computer.
■ Extend time on a patron computer.
■ Print a guest pass.
■ Send a message to a patron on a computer.
■ Add money to a patron's card.
■ Release a print job.
■ Reprint a print job.
■ Check the status of a computer.
■ Check the status of a patron.
■ Check the status of a session.

Event management software (if owned by the library)
- Register a patron for a program.
- Look up a program.
- Check program registrations.
- Cancel a patron from a program.
- Move someone from a waiting list.

Once staff members know what is expected of them, determine what training is needed to ensure they are competent. Training staff on technology competencies is much like training them on anything else. In order to properly train staff, the technology infrastructure needs to be in place so staff can be successful in their learning. If the Wi-Fi is constantly on the fritz, staff will never learn how to be confident in helping patrons log on because they won't know if it is them or the technology.

Having technology that people can try and play with is critically important. Make sure you have devices for staff to try and learn on. Once there are devices and equipment available, encourage (or even schedule) staff to play with them. The best way to learn about something is to try it out. Once they have experimented, engage them in more active learning and encourage them to teach each other.

When rolling out new technology to staff, provide structured classes on technology for staff to help them learn new products, equipment, or software. If the library just bought a new database, offer a training session so staff can learn about it. For databases, vendors will often provide webinars or send staff to do a training session. Also offer free time with an instructor in a room with computers or other equipment so that staff can drop in and ask questions or just play around. Some people feel more comfortable trying out new technology if they have someone there to whom they can turn with questions.

And, finally, make time for technology. If that means scheduling specific time each day or week for staff to devote to technology, then do it. They will become more vested in the library if the library invests in them.

LOOK TO THE FUTURE

Once you have a solid technology plan and trained staff, it is time to start thinking about the future. Ideally, there will be time to explore the future of technology in certain areas. In order to stay relevant, as library director, you need to be aware of current and future trends. Remember to take these steps:

1. Follow ALA's Center for the Future of Libraries.
2. Ask staff for feedback and ideas; they might be aware of something that you aren't.
3. Stay attuned to the community and goings-on in the schools, the chamber of commerce, village/city, park district, and so forth.
4. Never stop learning.

✿ REVIEW AND REFLECT

KEY TAKEAWAYS

Perform a technology assessment when you first arrive to get a big-picture view of where your library is at with technology, set up a plan for replacements, and plan for the future.

IT staffing can come in many forms and will depend on your library's individual needs. Some common staffing models are these:

- Dedicated on-site IT staff hired by the library
- Outsourced IT support for either some or all of the library's operating hours
- Vendor IT support that provides support on an as-needed basis
- Combo package that provides some combination of the above

Technology is always evolving. Ensuring you have staff trained in the core technology competencies is important to providing consistent support to patrons.

SELF-CHECK

- How much money did we spend last year on IT? What did we spend it on?
- Do we have a technology replacement plan?
- Where are all the IT passwords and log-in information stored?
- What large IT projects are coming down the road?
- Who handles the library's IT support?

QUESTIONS FOR REFLECTION

- What does the library need in terms of IT support?
- How much money should be set aside for IT annually?
- How often are passwords changed?
- What is the library's IT objective?

ADDITIONAL RESOURCES

⤓ **Download additional resources on our website at www.librarydirectorstoolkit.com/resources.**

American Library Association. "Center for the Future of Libraries." www.ala.org/tools/future.

———. "Other Technology Resources." www.ala.org/tools/librariestransform/other-technology -resources.

Berman, E. *Your Technology Outreach Adventure: Tools for Human-Centered Problem Solving.*
    Chicago: ALA Editions, 2018.

Breeding, M. *Library Technology Buying Strategies.* Chicago: ALA Editions, 2017.

Burke, J. J. *Neal-Schuman Library Technology Companion: A Basic Guide for Library Staff.* 5th ed.
    Chicago: ALA Neal-Schuman, 2016.

King, D. L. *How to Stay on Top of Emerging Technology Trends for Libraries.* Chicago:
    ALA TechSource, 2018.

11

STRATEGIC PLAN

After reading this chapter, you will know the following:

- How to decide whether to hire a consultant or go it alone in crafting a strategic plan
- What a mission statement is and how to craft one
- What a vision statement is and how to craft one
- How to plan and implement a successful strategic plan
- What types of community feedback methods are out there and how to use them in crafting your strategic plan
- What steps you need to take in approving, communicating, and implementing a strategic plan

reating a strategic plan, including the mission statement, vision statement, measurable goals, and action items, takes time and can be a lot of work, but it will help you lead your library into the future. Done well, crafting a strategic plan should take a few months at minimum. As the library director, you can facilitate the process yourself, with help from your staff and board, or hire a professional consultant. Regardless of who creates the plan, the process will be similar, but the length of time it takes will depend on how you structure your process. This chapter will help you understand the process and assist you in determining whether you want to undertake the process yourself or with a consultant.

A library should evolve as the world changes around it. In order to accomplish this, having a plan to follow is imperative. Strategic plans are usually created or updated every three to five years, with periodic reviews to ensure they are still relevant. A strategic plan allows your library to look at everything that the library could possibly do and narrows it down, through the lens of your mission and vision statements, to what you actually should be doing to move the library forward based on your community's needs. A mission statement is the foundation of a strategic plan and defines who you are; your vision statement defines where you want to go; your strategic plan tells you how to get there.

For directors and library boards, a strategic plan also helps you determine where to put your time, energy, and money in order to provide the services your patrons most desire. There are a number of components in creating a strategic plan. You will need mission and vision statements, input from stakeholders to gather data, and data analysis before finally creating the strategic plan based on measurable outcomes.

A CAUTIONARY TALE OF A LIBRARY WITH NO STRATEGIC PLAN

Anywhere Library has had three directors in four years. Because of this turnover, no strategic planning has taken place in years, and the old strategic plan sits on a shelf collecting dust. The library is in chaos. The board members are running the library as they deem necessary, changing policies whenever a patron complains. Staff never know from one week to the next what the policies are and what they are supposed to focus on beyond their day-to-day work. There is no formal interaction with the community to determine what they want from their local library. The staff orders whatever books they want because there is no formal collection development policy or clear budget. The finances are questionable at best. The library has enough money coming in but no written budget to follow. Any new director joining the library is going to be overwhelmed.

With no plan to work from, a new director will be trying to put out a lot of fires simultaneously with no clear direction. The policies are dictated by whomever complains. The collection is not being chosen based on what the community members want because they are not consulted in a formal setting, and programs are based on what staff find fun rather than what community members are interested in.

If a strategic plan were in place, the director, board, and staff would be utilizing that document when making decisions on policy, collections, programming, and event staffing. The library would query the community in a constructive manner instead of reacting to complaints made to individual board members by community members seeking change. Staff would have a clear vision of what they should focus on in both the day-to-day work of the library and for larger projects that help move the library forward. A formal mission statement would be in place along with a vision statement to help guide the library to where it is going.

HIRING A CONSULTANT FOR A STRATEGIC PLAN

Before starting the strategic planning process, you need to determine whether you want to craft a strategic plan on your own or with a consultant. If you choose to do it on your own, the process can be the same, except you are the one putting all the pieces together and formulating how you want to gather the data.

Why choose to go it alone? There are several reasons you might want to consider doing the plan yourself:

Time: You want to get a plan done quickly and can choose how long it will take to make that happen.

Control: You can decide what route you want to take and will hold the reins firmly in your hand.

Funding: You may not have the funding to hire a consultant.

Connection to the community: You may know the community well and can quickly identify the key people from whom you need to gather information.

But sometimes you might not want to do it alone, and so you can choose to hire a consultant. Here are several reasons you might want to consider hiring a consultant:

Time: You don't have enough of it, and you want to get a strategic plan in place.

Expertise: Hiring a consultant who only (or mostly) does strategic planning with libraries (or other organizations) means that you are hiring an expert who does this type of work all the time.

Objective view: A consultant can look at data and results one step removed, as opposed to your doing it internally and having to confront sacred cows that you won't feel comfortable touching.

Confidentiality: People may be more willing to speak candidly if they are speaking to someone who is not a staff member. Remember that you want honest feedback.

Do not assume, however, that by hiring a consultant you have removed yourself from the process. You will still be deeply involved in crafting the strategic plan. You are the one who is going to have to live with it, so you want to have a plan in place that works for you and your library. No matter how wonderful it is to have a consultant, at the end of the day, the consultant goes home and you stay. Working with a consultant is a partnership; you need to work together to make a plan that will help your library remain relevant to your community.

Another aspect to consider in hiring a consultant is cost. Depending on the process you use, hiring a consultant can cost anywhere from $2,000 to $50,000, or more, for a complete strategic plan.

What is the process for deciding to hire a consultant? First, you need to see if your board is open to hiring a consultant. If so, you can start to solicit proposals from strategic planning consultants. Talk to libraries in your area for recommendations on whom they have used and ask to see what their finished products look like. Look over these samples and ask about each consultant's process to get a feel for how each operates. This process can be quick or take a long time, depending on your board, your workload, and how pressing it is to move forward. Once you have a list of possible consultants, ask for proposals.

After reviewing the proposals, your board may want to interview the consultants or pick one or two to interview. The board may also just choose from the list of consultants who submitted proposals. When contacting consultants to bring to the board, remember to make sure that you can work with them. Also, consider their process. While the main framework is generally the same, different consultants might use different methods. Make sure that they will be a good fit with your library and that you feel comfortable working with them. If you can avoid it, don't ask for proposals from any consultants with whom you feel you can't work. Adding them to the mix will only make your life more complicated.

After a consultant has been chosen, that consultant will work with you, the board, and library staff throughout the planning process. The consultant will facilitate the focus groups and extract data and then analyze that data to find some common themes from which to create measurable goals. If hired for the entire process, the consultant will discuss overarching themes that arise from this analysis and work out an action plan for staff to implement.

PLANNING THE PROCESS

Whether you decide to hire a consultant or go it alone, there are many steps you will need to go through in order to craft a strategic plan that truly reflects your community's needs. While you may opt to skip some parts of the process, that approach can lead to a strategic plan that doesn't move the library forward or doesn't meet your community's needs.

To start, you will meet with your board to discuss in detail your planning process. If you plan to use a consultant, you will need to meet with the consultant to coordinate the plan. You will establish your mission and vision statements, determine your method(s) for querying the community, and set key dates for the different parts of the process. Create a timeline of all the tasks you need to undertake from conception to approval so that everyone is on the same page before, during, and after the process. Creating a detailed timeline also helps ensure you can measure your process along the way.

STEPS IN CRAFTING A STRATEGIC PLAN

1. Decide to hire consultant or plan internally.
2. Create a strategic planning committee (if applicable).
3. Craft or revise the library's mission statement.
4. Craft or revise the library's vision statement.
5. Solicit community feedback (usually the longest part of the process).
6. Analyze data from community feedback and internal statistics.
7. Set strategic plan goals.
8. Develop strategic plan action items.
9. Determine measurable outcomes for the action items.
10. Finalize the strategic plan, including mission, vision, goals, and action items.
11. Present the strategic plan to the board for approval.
12. Roll out strategic plan.

CRAFTING A MISSION STATEMENT

Once you have determined your process for creating a strategic plan, you will begin by focusing on making sure you have a strong mission statement for your library. A mission statement tells your patrons who you are and what you are about. It is the launching pad for your vision statement.

All members of your library, from the board to the staff, should know the library's mission statement and keep it foremost in their minds as they serve the community. Stop for a moment to see if you can recite yours or recall the last time it was mentioned by anyone in your library.

Before drafting or editing a mission statement, you, along with input from the staff and board, will need to define the library through answers to the following three questions:

1. Who are we?
2. What do we do?
3. Why do we exist?

Once you have answered these questions, try to combine those responses into a single statement. Your staff and board may want to craft the mission statement as a group. Avoid that scenario whenever you can. Draft a mission statement that can be tweaked as needed to avoid spending unnecessary hours changing one or two words.

Here are some samples of mission statements that reflect individual libraries' missions for their communities:

Dover (MA) Town Library: The Dover Town Library provides free and open access to materials and resources to educate and inspire all members of our community.

Indian Trails Public Library District (Prospect Heights, IL): We enhance the community and create opportunities through services, programs, and materials.

New York (NY) Public Library: To inspire lifelong learning, advance knowledge, and strengthen our communities.

Seattle (WA) Public Library: To bring people, information, and ideas together to enrich lives and build community.

Once you have written your mission statement, evaluate it. The evaluation process can involve the staff and board, but again, make sure only one person is doing the final editing, so you don't descend into wordsmithing hell. Ask these questions:

- Is the statement clear, concise, and realistic?
- Does the statement reflect your library's values and beliefs?
- Does the statement demonstrate a commitment to serving the public?
- Is the statement powerful?

Your mission statement should be about your library and reflect your community's needs. Based on your evaluation, make any necessary changes and rewrite. The following is a sample of a mission statement before and after the evaluation process:

Old mission statement: The XYZ Library provides access to the universe of information and makes it available to the community to promote the communication of ideas, to enlighten citizens, and to enrich the personal lives of all district residents.

New mission statement: XYZ Library: To inform, enrich, and enlighten.

CREATING A VISION STATEMENT

After you have crafted, updated, and reviewed your mission statement, you need to either review an existing or craft a new vision statement that tells your community where the library wants to go. Unlike a mission statement, which is the core of who and what you are, a vision statement is about considering the future and determining what path you want to follow to move your library into the future. It should change over time as the community changes and library services evolve to meet those changing needs. A vision statement could for a decade, or you might find it becomes obsolete in a few years.

The vision statement needs to be reviewed as part of your strategic planning process and should build upon your mission statement: where you are going should be based on who you are.

Here are several examples of powerful vision statements:

Dover (MA) Town Library: A place for all reasons.

Indian Trails Public Library District (Prospect Heights, IL): Embracing Culture. Connecting Community. Igniting Curiosity.

Red Hook (NY) Public Library: To create innovative opportunities that enrich the lives of Red Hook residents by providing information that inspires curiosity and leads to learning experiences for patrons of all ages.

Seattle (WA) Public Library: A city where imagination and opportunity thrive.

The vision statement should be the result of discussion and should, like the mission statement, be something that all staff and board members know. In crafting the vision statement, think ahead ten years to determine what type of library you want in the future and ask the following questions:

1. What image do we have of the library in the future?
2. What will distinguish the library from other community organizations?
3. What benefits can residents expect from the library?
4. How would you like people, especially nonusers, to describe the library?

Once you have answered those questions, craft the vision statement in the same manner as the mission statement. It should be concise and to the point. You may also have a longer document that accompanies the vision statement which describes in more detail what your vision means for your library and which often includes the answers to the previous questions.

GATHERING DATA AND COMMUNITY FEEDBACK

A community assessment should be part of any strategic plan. Your primary goal is providing the space, collections, services, and programs your community wants. You cannot do that unless you know what community members want. This is the boots-on-the ground, getting-dirty portion of the strategic planning process.

There are many methods that you can use to collect data from your community. Each has its own benefits and drawbacks and almost all of them can be done either by you and your staff or through a consultant, depending on the time and money you have available. Often a library will use a hybrid approach, employing different methods to gather information from different segments of the population. This is fine as long as the same questions are being asked so that you can do an apple-to-apple comparison.

FOCUS GROUPS

A focus group is a preselected group of people, usually picked based on demographics or interest levels, that meets to discuss their wants and needs. The types of groups are usually determined in conjunction with the board or consultant. The goal of the focus group is to provide an opportunity for the community to identify community needs and determine how the library is already meeting those needs or what gaps in coverage exist so the library can change its focus to meet the needs. Each focus group is asked the same set of questions in order to be able to compare responses.

Benefits

- You will gain feedback from a wider pool of people than is possible with one-on-one user interviews.
- You will get more in-depth answers about the wants and needs of your community.
- You can target specific groups of community members.

Drawbacks

- You may miss a target group that is critical to your community.
- You may have one or more people in a particular group who dominate the discussion.
- Identifying or soliciting users for the different focus groups can be challenging.
- Focus groups also require a fair amount of staff time, even if a consultant moderates the group.

KEY STAKEHOLDERS DISCUSSION

Identify key community stakeholders, such as school officials, chamber of commerce members, city/village officials, members of service organizations, or leaders of religious institutions. This is your opportunity to pick their brains about what are the overarching needs of the community. In this discussion, it is better not to focus on the library but rather on the overall community needs, and then you can talk about how the library can meet those needs.

Benefits

- You can get great information from a group of key people who see the community in very specific ways. They know what works and what doesn't and can share that with you.

- This is generally a fairly low-cost option. You can hold the discussion at the library and pay for only staff time and light refreshments.

Drawbacks

- Identifying the key stakeholders can be challenging if you are new to the community or if you have a very large community.
- The key stakeholders may not want to participate.
- There is usually some difficulty in finding a time when all of them can meet. As active participants in your community, these people are usually very busy.

ONE-ON-ONE INTERVIEWS

One-on-one user interviews can be a great way to get targeted information from different types of users. When choosing people to interview, you should seek out people who regularly use the library, key community stakeholders, and also some random people within the community. For the latter, you can go to a local grocery store, coffee shop, or shopping mall and ask people if they are willing to answer a few quick questions. It is helpful to query non–library users to find out why they don't use the library. Their responses may be very surprising and may present opportunities to serve an otherwise unserved segment of your population.

When doing one-on-one interviews, be sure to get basic demographic information on the participants so you can determine if different populations within your community have different needs. Use a list of preselected questions that will enable you to compare apples to apples when analyzing the data.

Benefits

- You will get targeted information from key people who are either prominent in the community or use the library on a regular basis.
- These interviews are much less expensive in terms of initial cost outlay. You need only a space to meet and a pen and paper (or a recorder) to document interviewees' answers.
- You have an opportunity to query non–library users as to why they don't use the library.

Drawbacks

- These interviews typically take thirty minutes each and then need to be transcribed and analyzed, so they are very time intensive for either staff or a consultant.
- You will not be able to get a large sampling of the community.
- Staff time or consultant time is expensive, so costs can add up quickly with this type of interview.

TELEPHONE SURVEY

Typically, you will hire an outside firm to administer a telephone survey by calling random people in your community to ask them a set of questions. This method can be very expensive, and you may not get a huge response. With the proliferation of robo calls and telephone scams in recent years, many people do not answer the telephone if the call is from an unfamiliar number, and others consider phone surveys to be intrusive. Companies that regularly conduct this type of survey maintain lists of phone numbers for the community. Be sure to check references for these companies if you decide to go this route.

Benefits
- You can talk to people one-on-one and hear what they are saying instead of guessing at their meaning from a written survey.
- You can reach library users and non–library users.
- You can hire an outside group to perform the survey if time is an issue.

Drawbacks
- Many people do not respond to this type of survey.
- Many people will not answer calls from unfamiliar numbers due to experience with robo calls and telephone scams.
- This type of survey can be expensive for the number of responses you end up receiving.

MAIL SURVEYS

A mail survey can be done using an outside firm, or you can handle this internally by creating a survey and mailing it out along with an SASE (self-addressed stamped envelope) to every home in your community so community members can fill out the survey and return it to the library.

Benefits
- You are offering an opportunity to comment to everyone in your community in the most direct way possible.
- You can possibly reach non–library users who will not see the survey any other way.

Drawbacks
- Mailing out a survey is expensive.
- Return rates, even when you include an SASE, can be low.

ONLINE SURVEY

You can create and easily share an online survey by posting the survey link through multiple channels, like the library's newsletter, website, and social media accounts. You can also ask your local schools, city/village government, chamber of commerce, and other local organizations to share the link on their social media sites to reach a larger audience.

Benefits

- You can go low cost or high cost depending on your funding.
- People may be more likely to complete an online survey because it can be quick, easy, and done on their own schedule.
- You can reach library users and non–library users.
- Many online survey companies are inexpensive and offer a built-in analysis tool to crunch the data once the survey closes.

Drawbacks

- You don't get to respond directly to people's questions or misinformation if they put in a comment that is inaccurate.
- There is the danger of having someone take the survey multiple times and skewing the results.
- If you don't carefully structure your questions, all the data you gather will be useless.
- Segments of your population may not have access to the Internet or possess the skills to complete an online survey.

INTERNAL DATA COLLECTION

Gather your library statistics to include in the overall strategic planning picture. When crafting a strategic plan, you need some cold, hard, reliable facts to help you determine how people are using your library and any past or future trends. Here are some different data points to consider:

Circulation: Who checks out materials at your library and what types of materials? Are your patrons using other libraries? Are other libraries' patrons using your library? How many interlibrary loan requests are sent and received?

Programming: How many programs do you offer? How many people attend your programs? What programs do you offer for what ages? Do you have program surveys that let respondents share their thoughts? What types of programs do people typically enjoy most?

Services: What services do you offer, who uses them, and how often? Do you offer nontraditional services (e.g., study room usage, computers, genealogy appointments), and if so, what are they? How do you track that information?

E-resources: What do you have? What is used, and what isn't?

Visitors: Who uses the library? What times of the day/days of the week are most/least popular?

Demographic information: Who lives in your service area in terms of age, nationality, economic situation, education, and so on?

When considering what data to gather, remember that no one piece of data will provide all the answers. The different categories allow you to put together pieces of a puzzle in order to see the big picture. If you do not have certain pieces, you can still put the puzzle together with the remaining parts.

Benefits

- You take away the personal aspect and just look at usage, which allows you to strip out many biases.
- You can see trends on data that you don't get from user interviews or surveys.

Drawbacks

- You need to have been collecting the data for a while to be able to use this method. If you are only just starting to collect the data or have changed how you are collecting it, you will not be able to use it to analyze trends over time.
- This is a tortoise situation, not a hare one. If you want to get something quick, data analysis is not going to give you what you want. It takes years to build up good data.

DEVELOPING THE STRATEGIC PLAN GOALS AND ACTION ITEMS

Once you have gathered all the data, you need to analyze that data. Are you finding patterns or themes in what has been gathered? Are there clear areas where the library is weak or strong? Focus on main areas that come up because of your research, and don't forget to look at the negatives. Ask yourself the following questions to get to the heart of the data:

- What are the broad topics (service to seniors, financial sustainability, community engagement, etc.) that come up in the research?
- What are the most important and the least important of those topics?
- What topics are impossible to address right now?
- What are the negative responses, and are there any similarities among those responses?
- What topics are we already doing, but maybe not in the way people want?

These patterns and the topics that come out of them help narrow your focus and are how you develop your goals, which will determine where you are going to focus your efforts for the next three to five years. Based on the topics you have identified, using words that fit your library and your community, develop statements that describe where you want to get to, your goals. Remember, these should also fit in with your vision statement, so refer back to that after each goal is crafted to see if the goal helps you achieve your vision.

Here are some example goals:

- Address community aspirations and concerns through sustainable partnerships.
- Support the economic vitality of our community.
- Define critical library outcomes and measure them annually.
- Develop additional funding sources to maintain the current level of service.

Once your goals are in place, work with your staff or management team to come up with your action items for accomplishing each goal. You don't want to bring any of this to the board at this point as the board will not be doing the work on the strategic plan. Your action items are going to give you the step-by-step instructions for what you will be spending your time on. Your action items should be SMART:

Specific: Action items should clearly define what you are going to do to achieve the goal.

STRATEGIC PLAN DOS AND DON'TS

What to do to craft a good strategic plan:

- Set clear goals that everyone on staff can get behind and remember easily.
- Include measurable action items that can be tracked and reported on to the board.
- Define clear outcomes that will show how you are moving forward.
- Include a limited number (three to five) of goals to focus on.

What NOT to do when crafting a strategic plan:

- Create a plan so complicated that no one wants to follow it.
- Have a plan that is so long that no one wants to work on it because it seems insurmountable.
- Craft goals that are so hard that none of the goals are achievable.
- Ignore it except for when the board wants an update.

Measurable: Action items should be measurable so you have a tangible way to determine if you have reached the goal.

Attainable: Action items should be achievable. You want to stretch yourself, but you also need to be able to accomplish the goal.

Relevant: Action items should fit in with the vision and mission of the library.

Timely: Action items should have start and end points. Make sure you know when you are doing a particular action item, from start to finish.[1]

You also want to consider what the outcomes will be for each action item. How will you know that this has moved you closer to the goal you have set? Now that you have defined your goals and action items along with the outcomes for determining if you have succeeded in moving the library forward, you are nearly finished. Remember that a strategic plan is a living document, and if your library's needs change, your strategic plan should change too. That can happen when you review the plan with your board each year.

APPROVING AND IMPLEMENTING THE STRATEGIC PLAN

Now that you have a completed strategic plan, the plan is ready for approval by your board. Your board may ask you to revise some of the goals or action items. Reviewing the strategic plan is one of the most important jobs your board does, and they are ultimately the ones responsible for answering to the community about where the library is going. Their feedback is key in ensuring the success of the plan.

Once any changes have been made and the strategic plan has been approved by the board, you need to share the plan with the library staff and your community. The goals should be discussed and placed at the forefront of the work that the library is doing daily. Talk about how the goals and action items relate to the library and to individuals within the library. Use the strategic plan as a guide when someone comes to you with a new program suggestion or other idea to determine if it fits into the mission, vision, and strategic plan of the library. Go over the plan regularly with managers and staff and discuss your successes and failures in carrying out the plan. Decide how you are going to share the plan and what you can do to keep it in the front of everyone's minds. Here are some questions to ask yourself when determining how to share and follow up on the plan:

- Who needs to know about the plan in the library and community?
- What opportunities do we have to share this information (e.g., all-staff meetings, board meetings, department meetings, etc.)?
- What is the best way to share the information in the plan?
- What visual aids are needed to keep the plan at the forefront of staff's minds?

- What do managers need to ensure the plan is incorporated into the departmental workflow?
- Do we need to create a slimmed-down version of the plan for a quick reference guide?
- How will we follow up on the plan with staff and board members?

Now you get to start on actually implementing the action items for all those goals you just set!

✿ REVIEW AND REFLECT

KEY TAKEAWAYS

Every library should have a strategic plan that lays out a plan for where the library needs to go.

You may choose to hire a consultant for a strategic plan, or you may choose to do the process yourself. Either way, you will be heavily involved in the crafting of a strategic plan.

These are the steps in crafting a strategic plan:

1. Craft or revise the library's mission and vision statements.
2. Solicit community feedback and analyze data from community feedback and internal statistics.
3. Set strategic plan goals and develop strategic plan action items.
4. Finalize the strategic plan, including mission, vision, goals, and action items.
5. Present the strategic plan to the board for approval.

Part of any strategic plan process includes gathering data and community feedback. This can be done in a variety of ways:

- Focus groups
- Key stakeholders discussion
- One-on-one interviews
- Telephone survey
- Mail survey
- Online survey
- Internal data collection

SELF-CHECK

- What is our library's mission statement?
- Do we have a vision statement? If so, what is it?

- Does our library have a current or past strategic plan? Where is it, and what is in it?
- Have we done any community data gathering? When? What were the results, and how were they used?
- What other ways does our library solicit or receive input from the community?

QUESTIONS FOR REFLECTION

- Does the library's mission statement reflect what the library is today?
- Does the library have a vision statement that reflects where the library wants to go?
- Do we have a strategic plan in place?
- How will we keep our strategic plan at the forefront in our day-to-day work?
- What is our plan to solicit input from our community going forward?
- Are the staff and board open to community feedback?

ADDITIONAL RESOURCES

See part II for these additional resources on strategic planning:

- Sample 11.1: Strategic Plan Visual Summary
- Sample 11.2: Mission Statement Worksheet
- Sample 11.3: Vision Statement Worksheet

⤓ **Download additional resources on our website at www.librarydirectorstoolkit.com/resources.**

Allen, B. *The No Nonsense Guide to Project Management.* London: Facet, 2017.

Gross, M., C. Mediavilla, and V. A. Walter. *Five Steps of Outcome-Based Planning and Evaluation for Public Libraries.* Chicago: ALA Editions, 2016.

IDEO. "Design Thinking for Libraries." www.ideo.com/post/design-thinking-for-libraries.

Nelson, S. *Strategic Planning for Results.* Chicago: ALA Editions, 2008.

NOTE

1. G. T. Doran, "There's a S.M.A.R.T. Way to Write Management's Goals and Objectives," *Management Review* 70, no. 11 (1981): 35–36.

12

WHAT'S NEXT?

After reading this chapter, you will know the following:

- ▪ Why you need to be a lifelong learner
- ▪ Why succession planning is necessary for the library director and library managers
- ▪ What should be contained in a succession plan document

‖‖

In the prior eleven chapters of this book, we discussed a variety of topics that will help any new library director through his or her first year. You now have a basic understanding of the key responsibilities of your job as a director:

Personnel: Hiring, training, supervision, evaluation, and termination of all the employees at the library

Board of trustees: Working with the board and ensuring board members are educated on the finances, strategic plan, programs, and services of the library

Finances: Preparation and execution of all facets of library finances

Legal matters: Serving as the main point of contact with the library attorney and ensuring the library is complying with all applicable laws

Policies and procedures: Drafting and implementing necessary policies and procedures to have a well-run library

Insurance: Managing the library's insurance policies

Building maintenance: Maintaining the library's facility

Emergency planning: Handling day-to-day emergencies and preparing plans for possible future emergencies

Collection development: Overseeing the collection, ensuring it meets the needs of the community, and appropriately funding collections

Programming and services: Making sure that the library offers a diverse range of programs and services to meet the wants and needs of the community

Community engagement: Attending community events and becoming involved in local organizations

Technology: Providing the technology your community needs and planning for future technology costs

Strategic plan: Carrying out the directives of the strategic plan after putting a plan in place

The previous chapters are a primer on how to get started as a library director, but they certainly are not the end of your learning journey. Being a library director is an extremely fulfilling job that is filled with daily challenges and experiences. Each of these challenges and experiences is a learning tool. However, to be an effective library director, you must continue to learn. Laws, trends, and best practices change, and as the library director, you need to be aware of these changes so that you can keep your library relevant. Ensuring continuing education for the library director, board, and staff is integral to a healthy library.

CONTINUING EDUCATION

The traditional forms of continuing education include reading professional books and journal articles, attending local meetings, and participating in state and national library conferences. In recent years, continuing education has become more accessible and less expensive (or free) than ever before. Now you can attend library school classes online, take e-courses, listen to podcasts, watch webinars, and attend MOOCs (massive open online courses). Many different e-learning sites for libraries are geared toward varying levels of knowledge and requirements.

As a library director, you need to understand legal and financial information, human resources, technology, project management, and a myriad of other topics. Participating in continuing education on non-library-related subjects will only enhance the work that you do.

The final piece of the puzzle in the work of a library director is making sure that the job you do is able to be done by someone if you are no longer there. The work of the library must go on, and you must find a way to ensure that happens.

SUCCESSION PLANNING

Succession planning is as important to an organization as having a capital improvement plan or an emergency plan. It does two things: (1) identifies and trains people within the organization who may be able to replace key staff members in the event that they leave and (2) creates a document that helps key personnel step in in the event of the absence of the director or manager.

Let's begin with identifying people within the library who may be best positioned to move into an administrative role if one becomes available. Library staff move on. Directors and managers retire or move to another library to advance their career, leaving a void in the management structure. The library may have current staff within the ranks who would be a great fit to become a department manager or director. They already know the culture of the library and are familiar with the staff, patrons, and community. However, these staff need to be groomed to take over a management position.

You and your management team should have discussions to identify any prospective staff for advancement. Have a conversation with said staff members to determine if they are interested and receptive to seeking additional training. Some people are not interested in management roles. That is okay. Staff members need to work where they are comfortable. If the staff members you have identified are interested in seeking additional training, create a plan on how to move that initiative forward. Depending on budget and library philosophy, the library may pay for any training, require the staff member to pay for his or her own training, or create a hybrid solution.

The goal of identifying and training current staff members is to position them to be the best possible candidates in the event of an open position at the library. You should make it clear that such positioning does not guarantee that the library will hire them for the open job, but it will put them in the best possible position to interview for it. Both the staff members and the library will benefit from any additional education and training they receive.

The second part of succession planning is creating a formal document that outlines the key aspects of the job. This document would be useful in the event that the library director or key managers leave or are not able to perform their duties for an extended period of time and someone else is put in place to run the library or a specific department.

While you adjusting to your new position, remember that keeping all the job-related information in your head will only lead to trouble down the road. Document how you do things so that others know how things are done and can fill in if you need to take an extended leave or for when you eventually decide to leave permanently.

SUCCESSION PLAN DOCUMENT FOR THE DIRECTOR

The library director is responsible for all aspects of the library and should have at least a basic knowledge of each department within the library and its procedures. However, this is likely not the case with the library director's job. Most library directors do their job and don't often share the intricacies with their staff. This can be an issue if the library director is unable to come to work for an extended period of time. It would be difficult for staff to pick up the workload without some information. This is why a succession plan is a good idea.

What should a good succession plan include? A library director's succession plan should have the following information:

- Log-ins and passwords for all e-mails, databases, and websites that are affiliated with the library director
- Bank information, including account numbers, log-ins, and passwords for all accounts and information on signatories for the accounts and how many are necessary to perform library business
- Library credit card information, including account numbers, log-ins, and passwords for all accounts
- Calendar of tasks to be completed by library director (likely to include the legal/financial filings and dates)
- Legal/financial filings and dates
- Sample legal/financial documents
- Library attorney contact information
- Library auditor and/or accountant contact information
- Any bond information (bond type, repayment schedule, etc.)
- Strategic plan
- Basic procedures for the position (bond disclosure, rate filings, etc.)
- Details of who takes charge if the library director takes an extended leave for three, six, nine, or twelve months (will likely need to be approved by the board of trustees).

Depending on the specifics of each director's position, this plan may be more or less extensive. The goal of the planning document is to provide a comprehensive list of the necessary information for anyone to be able to access the tools necessary to perform the basic day-to-day tasks of the library director.

SUCCESSION PLAN DOCUMENT FOR MANAGERS

As with the library director, there may be a time when a manager will be out for an extended period of time. The library director or another manager or staffer may need to step in to perform some of the managerial tasks. Thus, it is wise to create a similar document for management personnel.

The following information should be included in a manager's succession plan:

- Log-ins and passwords for all e-mails, databases, and websites that are affiliated with the manager's specific department
- Staff scheduling information
- Department calendar of events and programs that are specific to the department

■ Basic processes for the department (ordering books online, reviewing journals, interlibrary loans, creating library cards, etc.)

Depending on the specific duties of the department and manager, this plan may be more or less extensive. Given the nature of the data in the plans (log-ins/passwords), the information should be shared only with key personnel. The succession plan should not be made available to the general staff or entire board. Remember that the purpose of the plan is to have a blueprint in the event that someone needs to step into a position at the last minute.

Now that you have reviewed the tools needed for your first year as a library director, you have a solid foundation to build on as you move forward. While having this foundation is important, you will also find other resources that can help you in your journey as a director. Books, articles, conferences, and online learning will all be necessary, but the most important place to go for help is other librarians. We are a community that seeks to help one another. You are not alone. Reach out and ask for help. Someday, you will find yourself being the one to offer help. We are all in this together and are working toward making libraries the best they can be for our communities and the world.

✿ REVIEW AND REFLECT

KEY TAKEAWAYS

Continuing to learn is an integral part of being a library director. Be sure to allow time and funding in your budget to attend local meetings, seminars, conferences, and online offerings.

Another part of being a library director is to ensure that there is a succession plan in place for you and other key personnel in the event that you or they leave the organization. A succession plan should contain the following:

■ Log-ins and passwords for important accounts
■ Basic processes and procedures for the position
■ Any necessary job-specific details

And always remember that you are not alone.

SELF-CHECK

■ What continuing education opportunities are available for me and other staff?
■ Do I have a list of my log-ins and passwords in one place that would be easy for necessary staff to locate?
■ Have I, and my key staff, identified current staff who would be a good fit to move into a managerial position?

- Does my managerial staff have their log-ins and passwords in one place in the event I have to step in?
- What procedures do I need to document for my position? Staff positions?

QUESTIONS FOR REFLECTION

- Should I train key staff on certain functions of my job?
- Should I make sure that I can assume managerial roles and other managers are crossed-trained in each department?
- How much money should I set aside for continuing education for me and library staff?

ADDITIONAL RESOURCES

American Library Association. "Education and Careers." www.ala.org/educationcareers.
MOOC.org. "Massive Open Online Courses." www.mooc.org.

CONCLUSION

AS YOU HAVE JUST LEARNED, running a library is a big task, with many moving parts. We hope you now have a better understanding of what all those parts are and how they work together. From handling employee issues to advocating for your library in the community, you will wear many hats as a director.

As with any administrative-level position, it will have taken about a year for you to go through a full cycle of your responsibilities. While you have learned the basic responsibilities, we have discovered that we continue to learn throughout our entire careers. We hope you will as well. Lifelong learning ensures we are staying current and helps us not sit in an ivory tower, out of touch with our staff and patrons.

The second part of this book offers practical tools that you can start using immediately. You might find that some do not work for you. Luckily, we work in a field where people love to share. Ask your colleagues for sample documents. If you create something, share it with others.

Let the journey continue, and remember, you are not alone.

CONTENTS

PART II
TOOLS

SAMPLE 1.1

LIBRARY DIRECTOR TRAINING CHECKLIST

READ AND REVIEW

- ❏ Read one year of board minutes.
- ❏ Read one year of board packets.
- ❏ Read general policies.
- ❏ Read personnel policies.
- ❏ Review strategic plan.
- ❏ Review one year of library statistics.
- ❏ Review social media accounts for library.
- ❏ Read collection development policy.
- ❏ Review state laws pertaining to libraries.
- ❏ Review files of previous director, general administrative files, and personnel files.

MEETINGS

- ❏ Schedule one-on-one meetings with all direct reports.
- ❏ Schedule appointment with board president.
- ❏ Schedule one-on-one appointments with all board members.
- ❏ Set up meet-and-greets with staff during first month.
- ❏ Set up a meeting with any major vendors (e.g., IT, building, insurance) to learn about what they do for the library.
- ❏ Set up a meeting with the library attorney to introduce yourself and find out if there have been any recent issues.
- ❏ Set up a meeting with your auditor and go over the most recent audit.
- ❏ Set up meetings with village/city, park district, chamber of commerce, and so on, to introduce yourself.
- ❏ Set up meet-and-greets with patrons during first quarter.
- ❏ Contact your library consortium and ask for an orientation.
- ❏ Contact your regional library system and ask for an orientation.

- ❏ Contact your state library and ask for an orientation.
- ❏ Call neighboring library directors and introduce yourself.

VISIT

- ❏ Walk the library daily and jot down notes and ideas.
- ❏ Take a tour of each department and learn what projects each is working on.
- ❏ Drive around the town and learn about key places (e.g., schools, stores, park district).

OTHER

- ❏ Develop a communication plan.
- ❏ Sign up for e-mail discussion lists for library directors in your area.
- ❏ Sign up for community-wide notification services.

SAMPLE 1.2

DIRECTOR'S REPORT TEMPLATE

MONTH YEAR

AGENDA ITEMS

- Short description of each item on the agenda

TRUSTEE NOTES

- Including updates on things to remind the board and notes from individual trustees

BUILDING AND TECHNOLOGY

- Updates on issues and projects

STAFF AND VOLUNTEERS

- Staff arrivals, departures
- Volunteer work

CONTINUING EDUCATION AND MEETINGS

- Continuing education that staff members have attended
- Meetings the director has taken part in

COLLECTIONS AND MATERIALS

- Updates on new collections, processes, etc.

FINANCES

- Information about the audit, grants, etc.

PROGRAMMING AND OUTREACH

Adult Services

- Information highlighting some of the programs and outreach done in the community

Youth Services

- Information highlighting some of the programs and outreach done in the community

News and Marketing

- News articles, patron comments, etc.

OTHER

This includes anything that you feel doesn't fit elsewhere, such as a staff member having a baby, a funeral of a former staff member/trustee, legislative news, grant information, state library or library system news, and so forth.

NEW HIRE CHECKLIST

Employee Name/#: _____

Dept./Position: _____

Date of Hire: _____

- ☐ Initiate background check.
- ☐ Prepare offer letter.
- ☐ Remove job posting.
- ☐ Meet with new employee for orientation/tour.
- ☐ Issue keys.
- ☐ Process all new hire paperwork.
- ☐ Take picture of new employee.
- ☐ Add to medical insurance.
- ☐ Add to life insurance.
- ☐ Add to flex spending.
- ☐ Enter medical/dental/life coverage (or waive coverage).
- ☐ Prepare new hire packet.
- ☐ Create personnel file.
- ☐ Print time sheet (after staff accountant has entered eligible employee into database).
- ☐ Enter into new hire report.
- ☐ E-mail marketing department to welcome new hire in the weekly all-staff e-mail.
- ☐ Add to regional library system database.
- ☐ E-mail IT re: phone/voice mail setup and phone training.
- ☐ Upload picture into staff photo directory.
- ☐ Print picture and hang in staff lounge.
- ☐ Create label for mailbox.
- ☐ Order name tag.
- ☐ Enter new employee into database.
- ☐ Enter new employee into payroll worksheet.
- ☐ Follow up with employee regarding proof of car insurance.

SAMPLE 2.2

LIBRARIAN JOB DESCRIPTION

POSITION TITLE: LIBRARIAN
Classification: 9
Supervisor Title: Youth Services Manager
FLSA Status: Nonexempt

REQUIREMENTS FOR ALL EMPLOYEES

1. Pleasant personality, accurate in details
2. Ability to work with variety, change, and interruptions
3. Ability to communicate clearly
4. Ability to work effectively with patrons, coworkers, supervisors, and others
5. Ability to follow library policies and procedures
6. Ability to work independently

DUTIES CHARACTERIZED BY THIS CLASSIFICATION

Under the supervision of the Youth Services Manager, this employee is responsible for providing reference and readers' advisory services, participating in collection development and management discussions, and planning and presenting programs. Specific responsibilities/functions will be assigned by the Youth Services Manager on the basis of experience, skills, and specific needs of the department and number of hours worked.

REQUIREMENTS FOR THIS POSITION

1. Ability to communicate clearly and effectively with adults and children
2. Ability to establish and maintain effective working relationships with staff and public to achieve specific goals and objectives of the department
3. Ability to work independently and productively
4. Ability to develop and use effectively reference skills and practices
5. Thorough knowledge of general library philosophy, including the ALA's Library Bill of Rights

6. Ability to transform that knowledge into daily practice in the fulfillment of responsibilities
7. Working knowledge of library computer software systems and ability to problem solve and troubleshoot same
8. Working knowledge of the recreational reading interests and curriculum-related information needs of children preschool through young adult and their parents/caregivers

EDUCATION/EXPERIENCE REQUIRED

- Master of Library Science degree from an ALA-accredited school
- Working knowledge of library science theory and principles and of the organization of materials in the library
- Experience working with children and working knowledge of infant, child, and adolescent development
- Basic computer skills

KEY FUNCTIONS OF THIS POSITION

1. Provides reference services: working regular hours at the reference desk, using both print and automated resources, answering telephone reference questions, and developing a thorough knowledge of reference materials, tools, and techniques
2. Provides readers' advisory services: maintaining an awareness of bibliographies, indexes, and other tools that will assist in directing patrons to desired material; maintaining an awareness of topics of current or popular interest and popular authors; and reading regularly from selected areas and genres
3. Promotes the use of the collection: acquiring extensive familiarity with the collection; developing bibliographies as appropriate; and suggesting and/or helping to develop programs that promote or explain the use of library resources
4. Assists with program planning, promotion, presentation, and evaluation: developing and maintaining a knowledge of the developmental needs and interests of children of various age levels; and participating in the development of a balanced variety of educational and entertaining programs
5. Participates in appropriate local, state, and national professional organizations
6. Participates in appropriate continuing education activities: maintaining an awareness and understanding of current trends and issues in library

practices, technology, and philosophy; and developing and maintaining computer skills as required

PHYSICAL CAPACITIES

1. Frequent sitting, some walking
2. Lifting 35 lb; bending, stooping, climbing, pushing, and/or pulling up to 75 lb; reaching; handling
3. Vision for near and far

SAMPLE 2.3

UNPAID LEAVE OF ABSENCE POLICY

Occasionally, for personal or other reasons, you may need to apply for an unpaid leave of absence when you do not qualify for a leave under another of the library's policies and have exhausted all accrued leave. Under these circumstances, any staff member may qualify for a leave of absence. This leave of absence may be granted for a minimum of thirty days and a maximum of six months. Employees who take an unpaid leave of absence will stop accruing vacation and sick time until they return from the leave.

You must apply in writing for this leave of absence and submit your request to the Human Resources Manager. Your request should set forth the reason for the leave, the date on which you wish the leave to begin, and the date on which you will return to active employment with the library. The granting of a leave of absence, and the terms and conditions surrounding the leave of absence, are at the sole discretion of the library.

While the library makes every effort to reinstate the employee to his or her previous position, there are no guarantees.

Failure to return from a leave of absence at the time agreed will normally result in immediate termination of employment.

SAMPLE 2.4

SOCIAL MEDIA POLICY

I. GENERAL RULES AND GUIDELINES

The following rules and guidelines apply to the use of social media, whether such use is for the library on library time, for personal use during nonwork time, outside the workplace, or during working time while using library-owned equipment. These rules and guidelines apply to all employees.

1. Employees are prohibited from discussing confidential library matters through the use of social media. Confidential information means the library's patron account information, patron credit card information, and employee medical information. Employees may not post any information that is subject to attorney-client privilege.

2. Employees may not use social media to harass, threaten, libel or slander, bully, make statements that are maliciously false, or discriminate against coworkers, managers, patrons, vendors or suppliers, any organizations associated or doing business with the library, or any members of the public, including website visitors who post comments. The library's antiharassment and EEO policies apply to use of social media in the workplace.

3. This policy is not intended, nor shall it be applied, to restrict employees from discussing their wages, hours, and working conditions with coworkers.

II. LIBRARY-SPONSORED SOCIAL MEDIA

The library-sponsored social media is used to convey information about library products and services; advise patrons about events and updates; obtain patron feedback, exchange ideas, or trade insights about trends; reach out to potential new markets; provide marketing support to raise awareness of the library's brand; issue or respond to breaking news, or respond to negative publicity; brainstorm with employees and patrons; and discuss specific activities and events.

As such, the library-related social media is subject to the following rules and guidelines, in addition to rules and guidelines set forth above:

1. Only employees designated and authorized by the library may prepare content for or delete, edit, or otherwise modify content on library-sponsored social media.
2. Employees cannot post any copyrighted information where written reprint permission is not obtained in advance.
3. Designated employees are responsible for ensuring that the library-sponsored social media conforms to all applicable library rules and guidelines.
4. Employees who want to post comments in response to content must identify themselves as employees.

III. PERSONAL USE OF SOCIAL MEDIA

The following rules and guidelines, in addition to the rules and guidelines set forth in section I above, apply to employee use of social media on the employee's personal time.

1. Employees should abide by the Computer and Internet Usage Policy concerning personal use of the library's computer and related equipment.
2. Employees who utilize social media and choose to identify themselves as employees of the library may not represent themselves as a spokesperson for the library. Accordingly, employees must state explicitly, clearly, and in a prominent place on the site that their views are their own and not those of the library or of any person or organization affiliated or doing business with the library should they identify themselves as an employee of the library in a post. Employees may not refer to the library by name when publishing any promotional content and/or providing examples of any promotional content. This section does NOT prohibit employees from including the library's name, address, and/or other information on their social media profiles.
3. Employees should respect all copyright and other intellectual property laws. For the library's protection, as well as your own, it is critical that you show proper respect for all the laws governing copyright, fair use of copyrighted material owned by others, trademarks and other intellectual property, including the library's own copyrights, trademarks, and brands.
4. Employees may not advertise or sell library products or services through social media.

IV. EMPLOYER MONITORING

The library reserves the right to monitor employees' public use of social media including but not limited to statements/comments posted on the Internet, in blogs and other types of openly accessible forums, diaries, and personal and business discussion forums.

Employees should have no expectation of privacy while using library equipment and facilities for any purpose, including the use of social media. The library reserves the right to monitor, review, and block content that violates the library's rules and guidelines.

V. VIOLATIONS

The library will investigate and respond to all reports of violations of the library's rules and guidelines or related policies or rules. Employees are urged to report any violations of this policy to the Human Resources Manager. A violation of this policy may result in discipline up to and including termination of employment.

DISCIPLINARY POLICY

Should performance, work habits, conduct, or demeanor become unsatisfactory in the judgment of the library, based on violations either of the previous or of any other of the library's policies, rules, or regulations, an employee may be subject to disciplinary actions as follows:

- First Offense Verbal Warning
- Second Offense Written Warning
- Third Offense Disciplinary Suspension
- Fourth Offense Discharge

The library is not necessarily required to go through the entire disciplinary action process. Discipline may begin at any step, including immediate discharge (especially during the early stages of employment), dependent upon the severity of the incident. The progressive disciplinary steps and the failure to follow the steps in every situation do not in any way create a contractual right to continued employment.

Sometimes the library will find it necessary to investigate the infraction for which an employee may face discharge. In this case, the library may suspend the employee, with or without pay, pending the investigation. The objective of this suspension will be to determine if discharge is the proper decision. Following the investigation, if the library decides not to discharge the employee, the employee will be reinstated with or without back pay, depending on the circumstances.

TERMINATION CHECKLIST

Employee Name: _____

Dept./Position: _____

Last Day Worked: _____

Last Day of Employment: _____

Date of Final Paycheck: _____

- ❑ Request resignation letter from employee.
- ❑ Provide employee with exit questionnaire and schedule exit interview.
- ❑ Advise employee to call about pension (if applicable).
- ❑ E-mail manager to ask, Do you need access to terminated employee's e-mail or files?
- ❑ Move medical file from active to terminated.
- ❑ Complete any termination paperwork for pension and send in.
- ❑ Terminate and process personnel jacket on personnel file.
- ❑ Pull I-9 form from active binder; enter and file form in the terminated I-9 binder.
- ❑ Prepare and provide employee with COBRA letter (medical and/or dental).
- ❑ Delete from medical insurance.
- ❑ Delete from life insurance.
- ❑ Conduct exit interview (ask for personal e-mail and if last paycheck will be picked up or mailed).
- ❑ Collect employee handbook.
- ❑ Collect access card/keys.
- ❑ Enter unemployment information.
- ❑ Transfer benefit file to terminated section of cabinet.
- ❑ Remove from photo directory.
- ❑ Enter into position turnover report.
- ❑ Send IT ticket with requests:

    - ❑ Archive and remove accounts.
    - ❑ Transfer and archive drive files.
    - ❑ Deactivate access card.
    - ❑ Contact consortia and remove ILS log-in.

❏ Notify CIRC Manager (cc: CIRC Supervisor) of termination (name, department, and termination date) to delete staff library card/change to patron-only status.

❏ Notify Finance and Operations Manager to check if employee is registered for future dated seminars or conferences.

❏ Delete from regional library system database.

❏ Remove from phone list, emergency closing list, first aid certification list, etc.

❏ Remove name from mailbox.

❏ Remove from life insurance coverage, stop all accruals, and advise when last check will be issued.

❏ On final payroll run, include vacation due.

❏ Delete from Access database for current employees.

❏ Go into Access database for former employees; insert new record.

❏ Delete from car insurance list and pull declaration page from three-ring binder.

❏ Delete from payroll worksheet.

SAMPLE 2.7

||||||||||||||||||||||||||||||||||||||||||||||||||||||||||||||||||||||||||||||||||||||||||||||||||||||||||||||||||||||||||||

EMPLOYEE EXIT QUESTIONNAIRE

Date: _____

Name: _____

Department:_____

Job Title: _____

Date of Hire: _____

LAST DAY OF EMPLOYMENT

Voluntary: _____   Discharge: _____   Retirement: _____

Temporary: _____   Permanent: _____

If voluntary, what is the reason? _____

If temporary, when will you be returning? _____

FULL/REGULAR PART-TIME EMPLOYEES

Your group health insurance has been paid up to the month of: _____

Your group health conversion (COBRA) will cost: _____

Unused vacation hours to be paid out on last paycheck are: _____

Signed: _____

Date: _____

I. TRAINING

A. Did you feel your training was thorough enough to give you confidence in doing your job? _____

II. WORKING CONDITIONS

A. What did you like best or what did you feel was the greatest benefit working at the library? _____

B. What did you like least or find most difficult? _____

_____

III. PERSONNEL PRACTICES

A. Was your orientation for your position understandable and appropriate? _____

B. Was your pay level appropriate? _____

IV. MANAGEMENT

A. Did you feel you had a good working relationship with your supervisor? If not, why not? _____

_____

B. Did you feel you had a good working relationship with your coworkers? If not, why not? _____

_____

C. Did you take any complaints to your supervisor? If so, how was the complaint handled? _____

_____

D. Do you feel administration is responsive to employees' needs? _____

_____

E. Have you any further comments about your job, department, and/or supervisor or the library? _____

_____

F. What is the one major improvement to the library that you would suggest? _____

SAMPLE 3.1

TRUSTEE WELCOME LETTER

Dear Board Member,

Welcome again. Congratulations on your appointment/election to the library board. I look forward to working with you. Enclosed in this packet are some library goodies, board member and key library staff contact information, as well as information on completing the Freedom of Information Act and Open Meetings Act training, which is required for all new elected officials and must be completed within sixty days of being sworn in.

You will be receiving more information during the orientation, but before that happens, I want to share some basic information that you will hopefully find helpful.

Board meetings are typically on the third Thursday of the month at 7:30 p.m. in the meeting room. I will send out a request for agenda items at the beginning of each month. If you have anything that you would like added to the agenda, let me know, and we will include it on the agenda.

The board packet typically goes out the Friday before the board meeting. It is e-mailed out to all trustees and posted on the website. There are times when information is not included in the board packet online as it pertains to items that will be discussed in a closed session. Another item that is always e-mailed is the minutes from the previous month's meeting. They are then posted on the website after the board has approved them.

If you have any questions or want to discuss anything in the board packet or anything else, please do not hesitate to reach out to me. I will be in touch to schedule a convenient time to do your orientation.

I look forward to working with you.

Sincerely,
Your Library Director

LIBRARY BOARD VERSUS DIRECTOR ROLE

RESPONSIBILITIES	LIBRARY DIRECTOR	LIBRARY BOARD	FRIENDS
General Administrative	Administer daily operation of the library, including personnel, collection development, fiscal matters, physical building, and programmatic functions. Act as advisor to the board and provide support to the Friends and community groups.	Recruit and employ a qualified library director; maintain an ongoing performance appraisal process for the director in accordance with town charter.	Support quality library service in the community through fund-raising, volunteerism, and serving as advocates for the library.
Policy	Apprise library board of need for new policies as well as policy revisions. Present draft policies to the board and implement the policies of the library as adopted by the library board.	Identify and adopt written policies to govern the operation and programs of the library.	Support the policies of the library as adopted by the library board.
Planning	Coordinate and implement a strategic plan with library board, Friends, staff, and community.	Ensure that the library has a strategic plan with implementation and evaluation components.	Provide input into the library's strategic plan and support its implementation.

RESPONSIBILITIES	LIBRARY DIRECTOR	LIBRARY BOARD	FRIENDS
Fiscal Matters	Prepare an annual budget for the library in accordance with local laws.	Seek adequate funds to carry out library operations. Approve an annual budget for the library in accordance with local laws.	Conduct fund-raising to support the library's mission and plans.
Advocacy	Promote the mission of the library within the community. Educate the library board, Friends, and community regarding local, state, and federal issues that impact the library. Advocate for the library to legislators.	Promote the mission of the library within the community. Advocate for the library to legislators.	Promote the mission of the library within the community. Advocate for the library to legislators.
Meetings	Prepare for and participate in library board meetings. Ensure that there is a liaison from the board to the Friends, and vice versa.	Participate in all board meetings. Appoint a liaison to the Friends Board and become a member of the Friends.	Maintain a liaison to the library board.
Networking	Encourage the board and Friends to join state and national professional organizations and make them aware of educational opportunities.	Join state or national library associations as a resource for policies, operations, and advocacy for libraries.	Join the ALA's United for Libraries Friends of the Library chapter as a resource to better support the library.

SAMPLE 4.1

REVENUES BUDGET TEMPLATE

REVENUE	FY 2020 BUDGET ($)	% OF OVERALL BUDGET
Taxes		
Property taxes		
Replacement tax		
Interest income		
Federal/State		
Other		
Fines and Fees		
Lost/damaged items		
Nonresident fees		
Overdue fines		
Printing and copying		
Grants		
General		
Per capita		
Foundation or Friends		
Endowment		
Book sales		
Donations		
TOTAL REVENUE		

SAMPLE 4.2

|||||||||||||||||||||||||||||||||||||||||||||||||||||||||||||||||||||||||||||||||||||||||||||||||||||||||||||||||||

EXPENSES BUDGET TEMPLATE

REVENUE	FY 2020 BUDGET ($)	% OF OVERALL BUDGET
Personnel		
Salaries and wages		
Pension		
Group insurance		
Social Security		
Collections		
Books		
E-books		
Periodicals		
Databases		
Media		
Audiobooks		
Facilities		
Building maintenance		
Utilities		
Janitorial supplies		
Insurance		
Unemployment		
Property insurance		
Workers' compensation		
Liability insurance		

REVENUE	FY 2020 BUDGET ($)	% OF OVERALL BUDGET
Programming		
Programming		
Professional Development		
Professional development		
Contractual Services		
Legal		
Payroll		
Integrated library system		
Collection agency		
Consulting fees		
Audit		
Other		
Office supplies		
Internet/phone		
Postage		
Copy machines		
Hardware/software		
Marketing/public relations		
Furniture/fixtures		
Equipment		
Contingencies		
TOTAL EXPENSES		

PUBLIC CODE OF BEHAVIOR POLICY

The library welcomes all residents and visitors and is dedicated to free and equal access to information, knowledge, and independent learning for our diverse community.

The library seeks to provide its patrons, staff, and volunteers with a safe and pleasant library experience in an atmosphere conducive to connecting, studying, reading, creating, and learning. The library recognizes its unique position and responsibility to educate, inform, and enlighten the community through free resources, programs, and services that enable everyone to participate fully in our democratic society as members of a knowledgeable and educated citizenry.

With public service as the highest priority, the board of trustees has established the rules and regulations governing use of the library, such that all persons may enjoy its benefits. All library patrons can expect to

- receive courteous service;
- be treated fairly and equitably by all library staff;
- contact staff for reference, readers' advisory, and information services;
- have questions, comments, and concerns addressed in a timely manner;
- suggest new materials, programs, and services;
- have staff make the library operate in the best interests of the taxpayers; and
- have a safe, clean, and comfortable building.

Individuals visiting or using the library's facilities or services must comply with the following Public Code of Behavior. The library will uphold all federal, state, and local laws, rules, regulations, and ordinances in regard to public behavior.

1. Patrons shall be engaged in activities associated with the use of a public library while in the building.
2. Patrons may not interfere with the use of the library by other patrons or interfere with staff performance of their duties. Interference includes, but is not limited to,

   - use of loud, abusive, threatening, or insulting language or behavior, including language or behavior that offends, threatens, or insults groups or individuals, based on race, color, religion, national origin, sexual orientation, disability, or other traits;

- inebriation;
- activities or behavior that may result in injury or harm to any library patron or staff member, including challenging another person to fight or engaging in any fight; and
- photographing library users, volunteers, or staff without prior permission of the Executive Director.

3. Patrons may not sexually harass other patrons or staff. Harassment includes

   - making inappropriate personal comments or sexual advances;
   - using obscene or lewd language or gestures;
   - staring at or following a patron, volunteer, or staff member in a manner that reasonably can be expected to disturb the person; and
   - exposing others to sexual Internet content (more information on Internet usage can be found in the Internet Policy).

4. Solicitation is not allowed on library property. This includes selling, begging, or circulating petitions among patrons, volunteers, or staff members, except as otherwise allowed by law.

5. Patrons may consume food in the café area on the first floor. Covered beverages may be enjoyed throughout the library, unless otherwise indicated.

6. Bringing pets or animals, other than service animals necessary for disabilities, into the library is not allowed, except as authorized by the Executive Director for special programming purposes.

7. Shirts and shoes are required for health reasons and must be worn at all times.

8. Patrons whose bodily hygiene is so offensive as to constitute a nuisance to other persons shall be required to leave the building and may return when the problem has been corrected. Offensive body odor, poor personal hygiene, or overpowering perfume or cologne may require a patron to leave the building until such a time as the condition can become resolved.

9. Use of skateboards, rollerblades, or roller skates is not allowed in the library or on library property.

10. The use of incendiary devices, such as candles, matches, or lighters, is prohibited on library grounds. Smoking is not permitted within the library or within twenty-five feet of any public entrance.

11. Any other behavior that could reasonably be expected to disturb other users or interfere with the library staff's performance of their duties is prohibited.

12. While the library encourages use by everyone, it cannot assume responsibility for the care and supervision of any patrons who are disabled or impaired to the extent that they cannot independently follow library rules or be safe without a caregiver. Patrons who require personal supervision or assistance must provide this care themselves. In the event that a patron in the library requires such care and is without it, the library may contact social services or the police.

The above enumerated rules are not intended to be a complete list of violations but are intended for guidance only. Library staff and/or local law enforcement officers are authorized to expel persons who, advised of the regulations above, fail to comply with them. Such personnel also reserve the right to take appropriate action(s) against any other behavior which can reasonably be deemed to be offensive to library patrons or staff. Enforcement of these rules will be conducted in a fair and reasonable manner. Library staff designated by the director may temporarily suspend patron privileges for up to twenty-four hours, including restricting access to the library property, services, or programs for patrons who violate the public code of behavior. Unlawful activities will be reported immediately to the police.

SAMPLE 6.2

UNATTENDED CHILDREN AND VULNERABLE ADULTS POLICY

The library strives to provide a welcoming and safe environment for all community members. The library is particularly concerned for the safety of children and vulnerable adults on library premises.

While the library is concerned for the safety of children or vulnerable adults on library grounds, the library does not act in loco parentis (in place of parents). A parent, legal guardian, teacher, custodian, or caregiver is responsible for monitoring the activities and managing the behavior of children or vulnerable adults during their library visits.

Vulnerable adults are functionally, mentally, or physically unable to care for themselves and should not be left alone in the library, including at programs. This includes adults who need staff help beyond assistance with normal library services.

Children ten years of age and younger must be accompanied and directly supervised at all times by a parent or other responsible caregiver twelve years of age or older. These rules may apply to children over the age of ten at staff's discretion. Older children (age eleven and older) are welcome to use the library independently; however, responsibility for minors using the library rests with the parent/guardian. Children are subject to library rules and policies concerning behavior, conduct, and demeanor.

During library hours, when the safety of an unattended child or vulnerable adult is in doubt, library staff will attempt to contact the caregiver before calling 911. In the case of an immediate safety concern, staff will contact 911 immediately and then attempt to contact the caregiver. Staff will stay with the person until help arrives.

UNATTENDED CHILDREN AND VULNERABLE ADULTS AFTER HOURS

In the event a child under the age of fifteen or vulnerable adult is still at the library after the library closes to the public, the Librarian in Charge and one other staff member will wait fifteen minutes and then 911 will be called to take charge of the situation. Attempts will be made during that fifteen minutes to reach a caregiver or parent, but in no instance will staff take anyone home. If at any time staff are concerned for the safety of a child or vulnerable adult, they may contact 911 immediately.

GIFTS AND DONATIONS POLICY

1. Once a gift is accepted by the library, it becomes the property of the library, to be used or disposed of in accordance with the policies established by the board of trustees.

2. Except at the discretion of the Library Director or his or her designee, no special collections shall be accepted. All items added to the collection shall be integrated into the collection.

3. Gifts of money, real property, and/or stocks shall be accepted if conditions attached thereto are acceptable to the board of trustees.

4. Personal property, art objects, portraits, antiques, and related objects may be accepted. At the discretion of the board and the Library Director, property that is more properly described as museum objects will not be accepted.

5. The library will not accept for deposit materials that are not outright gifts. The library staff is unable to place a value on gift books donated to the library. For income tax purposes, the value of books donated shall be determined by the donor.

6. While gifts to the library as a governmental unit qualify as tax deductible, donors should seek the tax advice of counsel or their accountant.

SAMPLE 7.1

||||||||||||||||||||||||||||||||||||||||||||||||||||||||||||||||||||||||||||||||||||||||||||||||||||||||||||||||||||||||||||||||||||||||||||||||||||||

INCIDENT AND ACCIDENT REPORT FORM

Use this form to record information during an incident.

Your name: _____

Date: _____ Time: _____ ❏ AM ❏ PM

Incident location: _____

Did this incident happen to: ❏ Patron(s) ❏ Staff

Did this incident involve any of the following? Check all that apply.

❏ Alarm   ❏ Meeting rooms
❏ Building emergency (fire, etc.)   ❏ Damage to building
❏ Accident   ❏ Parking lot
❏ Injury   ❏ Patron behavior
❏ Illness   ❏ Other (specify): _____

Was 911 called? ❏ Yes ❏ No

Police Report Number: _____

Patrons directly involved (include contact information): _____
_____
_____

Patron witnesses (include name and phone number): _____
_____
_____

Staff witnesses (include name and phone number): _____
_____
_____

Describe the incident. Remember to be objective and factual. Please use the back if needed. _____
_____

_____

_____

_____

_____

_____

Your actions or response: _____

_____

_____

_____

Follow-up or additional actions needed: _____

_____

_____

_____

Additional comments from the Librarian in Charge: _____

_____

_____

_____

Librarian in Charge signature: _____

SAMPLE 8.1

LIBRARY CLEANING CHECKLIST

GENERAL LIBRARY AREAS (entry, meeting room, children's area, study area, main collection area, computer lab, reading area)	DAILY	WEEKLY	MONTHLY	2X PER YEAR	ANNUALLY
Empty trash receptacles; pick up trash on floors or tabletops.	X				
Dust or wipe down tabletops and chairs.	X				
Vacuum carpets, including under tables/desks, and high-traffic mats.	X				
Vacuum and mop all hard floor surfaces.	X				
Sanitize all water fountains.	X				
Wipe fingerprints/smudges off doors and windows.	X				
Clean entrance doors and windows.	X				
Dust high/low areas and remove cobwebs.		X			
Dust ceiling vents/grills.			X		
Scrub ceramic tile floors.				X	
Clean tile grout.					X
Restrooms (public and staff)					
Empty all trash receptacles.	X				
Thoroughly sanitize sinks, commodes, urinals, countertops, partitions, grab bars, changing tables, and wall areas by dispensers.	X				
Restock paper products.	X				
Clean mirrors and all faucets/knobs/handles.	X				

GENERAL LIBRARY AREAS (entry, meeting room, children's area, study area, main collection area, computer lab, reading area)	DAILY	WEEKLY	MONTHLY	2X PER YEAR	ANNUALLY
Sweep/vacuum/mop all floors.	x				
Sanitize all doors and handles into restrooms.	x				
Sanitize hand dryers.	x				
Kitchen Areas (meeting room and staff)					
Empty trash receptacles.	x				
Restock paper products.	x				
Thoroughly sanitize sinks and faucets.	x				
Wipe down outside of refrigerator.	x				
Clean inside and outside of microwaves.	x				
Wipe down all tabletops.	x				
Wipe down chairs and table pedestals.		x			
Clean out refrigerator.			x		
Sweep/vacuum/mop floors.	x				
Staff Offices/Desks					
Empty trash receptacles.	x				
Gently dust/wipe down desks, taking precautions not to move any papers.	x				
Clean smudges from doors, frames, and interior windows.	x				
Dust bookshelves gently, taking precautions not to move books and other items on shelves.		x			

SAMPLE 9.1

STAFF EMERGENCY RESPONSES

In an EMERGENCY situation, act immediately and call the police, describing the situation. Police will determine how to handle the situation.

In a NON-EMERGENCY situation, you will need to use your own judgment. If patron or staff rights are being violated, enforce the Rules of Patron Deportment as set by the board of trustees.

The following chart is to be used as a guide to dealing with emergencies; for more complete instructions, go to the guidelines for that emergency.

EMERGENCY
Time is critical. Danger of physical harm to staff or patrons.

Type of Situation	What to Do	When to Do It	Who Does It
Fire	1. Call 911. 2. Notify Person in Charge. 3. Evacuate building.	Immediately	First person aware of situation
Severe weather ▪ Weather warning ▪ Tornado watch ▪ Tornado warning ▪ Winter storm	▪ Monitor radio and fax for updates—follow emergency plan. Check online weather services.	Immediately	Person in Charge
	▪ Listen to radio for updates—follow emergency plan.	Immediately	Person in Charge
	▪ Notify staff and patrons to move to safe area—follow emergency plan for announcement script.	Immediately	Person in Charge
	▪ Listen to radio for updates—follow emergency plan for closing procedures.	Monitor	Person in Charge in consultation with board president

Power outage	1. Call electric company to report outage. 2. 2a. *In daylight:* The Person in Charge may decide to keep the building open for up to sixty minutes depending on emergency lighting levels. 2b. *After dark:* Close the building immediately using standard closing procedures.	*In daylight:* Stay open up to sixty minutes depending on emergency lighting levels. *After dark:* Close immediately.	Person in Charge
Gas leak	1. Call 911. 2. Evacuate building. 3. Call gas company from outside the building.	Immediately	Person in Charge
Water main break	Call city/village.	Immediately	Person in Charge

UNATTENDED CHILDREN

OVERVIEW

Responsibility for the care and safety of the children using the library rests with the parents, guardians, or assigned caregivers, not with library staff. While the library assumes no responsibility for children left unattended, staff shall observe the following actions.

ACTIONS

Closing time:

1. Before closing, staff will check for unattended children and make sure they have a ride home. If they do not have a ride, staff will contact an adult to pick them up, making sure to tell the adult that police will be called if the child is here fifteen minutes past closing.
2. At closing time, if a child twelve years or younger is still here unattended, staff will contact the Person in Charge.
3. The Person in Charge and one other person of his or her choosing will wait with the child until fifteen minutes past closing. Staff will try to call the parents/guardians to come pick up the child.
4. If the parents/guardians are reached and request that the child be allowed to walk home, staff will fill out an Incident Report with this information.

5. Once fifteen minutes have passed, staff will call the police nonemergency number and request that police pick up the child at the library.
6. Library staff or police will inform the parent, guardian, or caregiver of the library's policy regarding unattended children.
7. If police pick up the child, staff will post a notice on the front and back doors that the child was taken to the police department. DO NOT POST THE NAME OF THE CHILD.

REMINDERS

1. Under no circumstances will library staff transport a child or take a child away from the library.
2. Two staff members must stay with an unattended child.
3. In the event of repeated incidents, the library should send a letter to the parent, guardian, or caregiver (certified mail, return receipt) that states the library policy regarding unattended children and informs the individual(s) that if the child is again left unattended, the police will be notified immediately and the township social worker will be contacted.

VULNERABLE PATRONS

OVERVIEW

In emergency situations, vulnerable patrons or patrons with disabilities may not have access to the elevators.

ACTIONS

In the event of an emergency, staff members in each department will check their assigned areas to make sure that all patrons are able to evacuate the building. Staff will assist any patrons with disabilities or special needs to safely exit the building using the stairs and emergency exits.

If you have multiple floors and there are patrons who are unable to exit using the stairways, staff will immediately call 911 and the Person in Charge and inform them of the specific location(s) of the patron(s). The Person in Charge should be informed as quickly as possible of any change in patron location(s). The Fire Department should be notified immediately upon their arrival of the location(s) of patrons with disabilities.

FIRE

On the second floor, patrons with disabilities who are unable to exit using the stairways should be assisted to the emergency stairwells.

The Person in Charge should be informed immediately if there are patrons being assisted from the second floor so that the Person in Charge can inform arriving Fire Department personnel. The Person in Charge should be informed as soon as possible of any changes in the location(s) of patrons with disabilities.

TORNADO/SEVERE WEATHER

If the warning sirens sound or if weather conditions seem extremely threatening, the Person in Charge should use the PA (public address) system to announce the weather emergency and instruct patrons to take their personal belongings and move quickly and calmly to the hallway by the boardroom.

The Person in Charge should also announce that any patron needing assistance in proceeding to the first floor should go immediately to the nearest service desk. Staff should contact 911 and inform them of any patrons needing assistance.

Staff will assist and/or accompany patrons with disabilities or special needs to proceed down the stairs to the hallway.

If safe evacuation to the first floor via the elevator is not possible and patrons are unable to use stairs to exit the second floor, call the Fire Department.

POWER OUTAGE

If there is a power outage and there are patrons with disabilities on the second floor who may need assistance should the library close, inform the Person in Charge.

If the library does close, library staff should announce that anyone needing assistance in exiting the building should inform the staff.

Staff should assist patrons with disabilities or special needs to contact transportation as required.

Staff should accompany any patrons needing assistance walking down the stairs, using flashlights for additional light if needed.

The Fire Department should be called to assist in evacuating patrons in wheelchairs or those who are unable to use the stairs safely to exit the building.

Staff should use judgment when a power outage occurs in the evening or when there is limited light. The Fire Department should be called for assistance when there is any question about patrons safely exiting the building using the stairs due to low vision or other disabilities.

Patrons with disabilities will not be asked to vacate the building with other patrons if additional time is required to allow them to safely exit the library. Under no circumstances should patrons be allowed in an area of the library without staff presence. Maintenance/security staff and the Person in Charge will remain with patrons until all are able to safely leave the building.

REMINDERS

Unless there is an extreme emergency where immediate exit from the second floor is critical (life-threatening situations such as fire or tornado), the Fire Department recommends that library staff wait until Fire Department personnel are able to assist patrons with disabilities. If a life-threatening situation exists, contact the Fire Department immediately.

STRATEGIC PLAN VISUAL SUMMARY

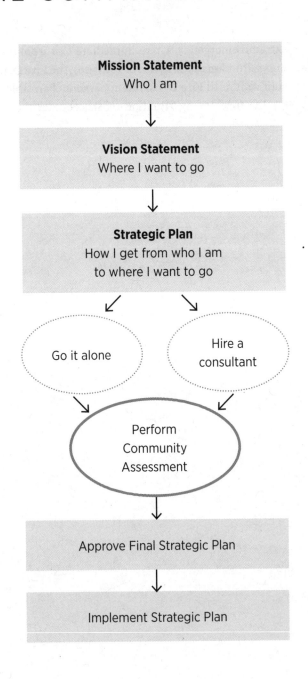

Mission Statement
Who I am

↓

Vision Statement
Where I want to go

↓

Strategic Plan
How I get from who I am
to where I want to go

Go it alone   Hire a consultant

Perform Community Assessment

Approve Final Strategic Plan

↓

Implement Strategic Plan

SAMPLE 11.2

MISSION STATEMENT WORKSHEET

Definition: A mission statement is a formal, short, written statement of the purpose of an organization. The mission statement should guide the actions of the organization, spell out its overall goal, provide a sense of direction, and guide decision making.

The mission statement should be a concise statement of organizational strategy, developed from the patrons' perspective, and it should fit with the vision for the organization.

A mission statement should be simple. The statement needs to capture the essence of what the library will achieve and how the library will achieve it.

The mission statement should be short and concise. The fewer words the better. Use just enough words to capture the essence. Most mission statements are too long. People tend to want to add additional information and qualifications to their base statement. Usually these statements just confuse the reader and cloud the real meaning of the mission statement.

Mission statements should be a single thought that can easily be carried in the mind and guide the everyday activities of every person involved in the organization.

Here are some examples:

New York (NY) Public Library: "To inspire lifelong learning, advance knowledge, and strengthen our communities."

Chicago (IL) Public Library: "Read, Learn, Discover!"

Orange County (FL) Library System: "Information, Imagination, Inspiration."

Daly City (CA) Public Library: "Preserving Yesterday, Informing Today, Inspiring Tomorrow."

Denver (CO) Public Library: "To help the people of our community to achieve their full potential."

Before drafting a mission statement, you need to define the library by answering the following questions:

1. Who are we?
2. What do we do?
3. Why do we exist?

Now take your responses from these questions and put them into a single statement:

_____
_____
_____
_____
_____

EVALUATE YOUR STATEMENT	Yes	No	Somewhat
The statement is realistic.			
The statement is clear and concise.			
The statement reflects our values and beliefs.			
The statement demonstrates a commitment to serving the public good.			
The statement is powerful.			

Based on your evaluation of the statement, jot down possible changes that you can make. Now, rewrite your statement based on those changes.

The mission of our organization is:

_____
_____
_____
_____
_____

SAMPLE 11.3

VISION STATEMENT WORKSHEET

Definition: A vision statement serves as a guideline for future strategic decisions. It simply answers the question, "Where do we want to go?"

The vision statement is a description of the library's "desired future state." Thus, a vision statement should describe the library as the board would like it to be. Note the emphasis on the future. The vision statement isn't true today; rather, it describes what the library would like to become—in the future.

The following are some guidelines on the qualities a vision statement should have:

Imaginable: The vision statement conveys a picture of what the future will look like. It is like painting a picture with words. It is an image that people can carry around in their heads.

Desirable: The vision statement appeals to the long-term interests of anyone who has a stake in the organization. It is a vibrant, engaging, and specific description of what it will be like to achieve the vision. Passion, emotion, and conviction are essential parts of the vivid description.

Feasible: The vision statement comprises realistic, attainable goals. It has a clear finish line.

Focused: The vision statement is clear enough to provide guidance in decision making.

Flexible: The vision statement is general enough to allow individual initiative and alternative responses in light of changing conditions.

Communicable: People get the vision statement right away; it requires little or no explanation.

Visionary: The vision statement will not be a sure bet—it will have only a 50 to 70 percent probability of success—but everyone must believe the goal can be reached anyway.

Here are some sample vision statements:

Charlotte Mecklenburg (NC) Library: "Aspires to be America's best public library."

> *Riverside (CA) Public Library:* "To be the foremost promoter of self-directed lifelong learning. We spark curiosity and provide tools for discovery."
>
> *Grand Rapids (MI) Public Library:* "To be our community's foremost source for information, viewpoints, resources and programs."
>
> *Dearborn (MI) Public Library:* "To foster the spirit of exploration, the joy of reading, and the pursuit of knowledge for all ages and cultures starting with the very young."

To craft a vision statement, you must first develop a vision of what type of library you want to have in the future. Think forward about ten years and answer the questions below.

- What image do you have of the library in the future?
- What will distinguish the library from other community organizations?
- What benefits can residents expect from the library?
- How would you like people, especially nonusers, to describe the library?

EVALUATE YOUR STATEMENT	Yes	No	Somewhat
The statement is realistic.			
The statement is clear and concise.			
The statement reflects our values and beliefs.			
The statement demonstrates a commitment to serving the public good.			
The statement is powerful.			

Based on your evaluation of your vision statement, jot down possible changes that you can make. Now, rewrite your statement based on those changes.

The vision of our organization is:

INDEX

Page numbers followed by "*t*" indicate tables.

R

record retention policies, 35, 65
recovering from emergency, 113–116
references, candidate, 19–20
reflection questions, 13–14, 27, 39, 56, 70,
    80, 95, 106, 117, 129, 146, 152
relationships
  with board of trustees, 37–38
  building, 9
reserve fund, 44, 51–52
responsibilities
  core, 3–6, 12–13, 147–148
  trustee, 29–33, 38
retainers, 62
revenues, 41–44, 42t, 177

S

salary schedules, 20–21
Sannwald, William, 49
scope of work, 68
self-checks, 13, 27, 39, 56, 70, 80, 95, 106,
    117, 129, 145–146, 151–152
service contracts/vendors, 98, 102. *See also*
    contracts/contractual accounts
services. *See* programming and services
severe weather, 192
shutoff valves, 99
social media policy, 166–168
staff emergency responses, 189–193
starting out
  core responsibilities, 3–6
  first year, 6–11
  work-personal life harmony, 11–12
state funding, 43
state laws, 63–65
strategic plan
  approving and implementing, 144–145
  board of trustees and, 30, 31, 144
  dos and don'ts for, 143
  goals and action items for, 142–144
  hiring consultant for, 133–134
  mission statement and, 135–136
  overview of, 6, 131–132
  planning process for, 134
  review of, 145
  vision statement and, 136
  visual summary of, 194
succession planning, 148–151
sunshine laws, 65
surveys, 140–141

T

taxes, 41, 43
technology
  assessment of, 119–121
  competencies with, 124–128
  creating plan for, 121–122
  future of, 128
  overview of, 6, 119
  review of, 129
  staffing for, 122–124
telephone surveys, 140
termination, 25–26, 27, 170–171
tornadoes, 192
training, 22, 79, 116–117, 128, 149, 157–158.
    See also continuing education
treasurer's bond, 91
trustees. *See* board of trustees

U

umbrella policy, 90
unattended children, 183, 190–191
unemployment insurance, 65, 91–92
unpaid leave of absence policy, 165

V

vendors, 11.
    See also contracts/contractual accounts
vision statement, 132, 136, 197–198
vulnerable patrons, 183, 191

W

warranties, 68
workers' compensation, 65, 92
working conditions, 18
work-personal life harmony, 11–12